D0918913

# Democratic Socialism

*Theory and Practice*

# Democratic Socialism
## Theory and Practice

MIHAILO MARKOVIĆ
*Professor of Philosophy, University of Belgrade*

THE HARVESTER PRESS · SUSSEX
ST. MARTIN'S PRESS · NEW YORK

First published in Great Britain in 1982 by
THE HARVESTER PRESS LIMITED
*Publisher: John Spiers*
16 Ship Street, Brighton, Sussex

and in the USA by
ST. MARTIN'S PRESS, INC.
175 Fifth Avenue, New York, N.Y. 10010

© Mihailo Marković, 1982

*British Library Cataloguing in Publication Data*

Marković, Mihailo
  Democratic socialism.
  1. Socialism
  I. Title
  335'.001      HX44
  ISBN 0-7108-0387-7

*Library of Congress Cataloging in Publication Data*

Marković, Mihailo, 1923–
  Democratic Socialism.

  1. Communism and society.   2. Communist state.
3. Social change.   I. Title.
HX542.M2976   1982      321.9'2      81-21283
ISBN 0-312-19383-1                   AACR2

Typeset by Inforum Ltd, Portsmouth
and printed in Great Britain by
Mansell Limited, Witham, Essex

All rights reserved

# Contents

# Preface

Whatever one might think about socialism, one thing is certain: the concept has never been so ambiguous and the status of what it stands for has never been so contradictory.

Societies that label their régimes as 'true socialism' emerged, at least in some cases, from real revolutions. They improved the lot of the poor, accelerated industrialisation and urbanisation, and turned millions of illiterate peasants into well-schooled and trained employees of the State. The traditional distinction between civil and political society disappeared. Socialism became a synonym of State-rule over the whole of social life. The State claimed to be something very special and entirely new: a workers' State, an extended hand of the people – but this was an iron hand, and it ruled mercilessly. Nothing helped capitalism so much as the fact that the only visible alternative looked so unappealing. The battle cry of revolutionaries: 'Socialism or barbarism' was given an effective reply: 'Socialism *is* barbarism. Socialism *is* Gulag.'

There is a long, tragic history of how it ever became possible to identify a noble vision of a more free and just society with a system of slave labour, and how this identification ever became credible. It would be illuminating to find out if there were flaws in the vision from the beginning, how it was moulded in the process of its interpretation and application under adverse conditions, and which social factors made it unattractive in some of the most developed countries of the world.

From earliest anticipations to the socialist utopias of Saint-Simon, Fourier and Owen, the emphasis was more on social justice, equality, collectivisation of productive forces, obligation of work for all, rational social organisation and social control in the general interest, than on individual freedom, personal self-fulfilment, humanisation of work, and of all social life.

Marx was a true philosopher of human emancipation: he

blended socialism and participatory democracy, utopian socialist critique of capitalism and anarchist critique of the State. Socialism, in his view, was possible only on the ground of highly developed bourgeois society with its advanced level of economic productivity and political liberty and the wealth of human needs. There was a number of ambiguities in his conceptions, but one had fatal consequences – that was his view that a transition period was needed between capitalism and the new society, that during that period all the necessary social transformation and repression of counter-revolutionary forces would be executed by a workers' State, and that this temporary workers' State would be characterised by a *dictatorship of the proletariat*. It was later forgotten that the term was used only to denote a temporary coercive rule of the working majority of people, which had to give way to a Stateless society, organised as a federation of workers' associations. The word 'dictatorship' was, however, well remembered.

Marx described fully the conditions under which the socialist project would be realised. But these conditions did not obtain, either in his own time or several decades after his death.

Western capitalism was able to continue to develop, to raise the overall standard of living, and to preserve its legitimacy in spite of repeated crises. Consequently, the socialist movement had to adopt reformist strategies.

Eastern Europe, on the other hand, had not yet reached the point of take-off for bourgeois modernisation. In those stagnant, rural societies, saddled with semi-feudal, authoritarian institutions, weak, parasitic upper classes, national conflicts and senseless wars, socialist revolution appeared a possible way out. Paradoxically, Marxist socialism became a tool of accelerated industrialisation, and building an essentially bourgeois consumer-society without bourgeois liberties.

Revolutions in those societies were inspired and led by small, clandestine, extremely disciplined and efficient organisations. Under given conditions nothing else was possible. What was possible sufficed for making a revolution and winning political power, but not for building radically new human relations. An authoritarian and hierarchical structure of the revolutionary vanguard could not but be reproduced in the entire society: only a democratic movement can produce a democratic society.

Claims to socialism were made in a society that in many important respects (the level of technology and productivity of work, political and cultural freedom) found itself below the level of advanced bourgeois society. This helped the latter to stabilise itself, to present itself as a free, efficient, civilised society and not only to survive but to continue to grow beyond any reasonably set limits. In the most developed Western countries, socialism seemed irrelevant and an increasingly dangerous threat. Irrelevant, since capitalism appeared to be endlessly able to deliver goods, and since the white, industrial workers more and more perceived themselves as a middle class, with various ethnic minorities at the lower rungs of social hierarchy. Socialism, in spite of its commitment to eternal peace, was seen as an external threat once its leading powers began to use force in international relations, to extend its systems to the world and to justify this sort of militant nationalism with the doctrine of proletarian internationalism.

And yet just at the time when even serious Western liberal intellectuals began openly to slide toward the Right, and to dismiss socialism as historically obsolete, two events occurred that shed new light on the entire issue of socialism.

In Poland in 1980–1 it turned out that the proletariat was able, after all, to assume the role of a revolutionary subject; that it could organise itself without the tutorship of any political party; that even under most difficult conditions, in a society without any democratic tradition, fully encircled by watching self-appointed brothers, menaced continually by armed intervention, workers, together with intellectuals and peasants, were able to create a grass-root democratic movement of an essentially socialist character. It is true (and shows the depths of the crisis) that *Solidarity* is sceptical of Marxism, does not profess any ideology, and even the word 'socialism' has been bracketed (which only shows how compromised it is now). Nevertheless, all basic values of the activists of *Solidarity* stem much more from socialism than fron any other tradition: solidarity, social justice, equality, human dignity, freedom from oppression and exploitation, abolition of privileges, the right to participate in social decision-making, a truly collective ownership of the principle means of production, control of all officials, and cultural creativity.

This can mean only one thing: in spite of all abuses and

travesties of modern socialism there is something in its spiritual tradition that can still inspire, that can give a sense of direction even to ardent Catholics, and the victims of an imposed pseudo-revolution, and of a pseudo-socialist system.

Another recent event of extraordinary importance was the electoral triumph of the French socialists. If one is aware of what entirely new and historically important possibilities are opened with this victory in one of the most developed, mature and most consistently democratic countries in the world, one must try to understand how what happened was possible. What made a large segment of the French middle class vote for a coalition that will most certainly introduce structural changes, nationalise many businesses, and then introduce self-government?

The strongest, serious argument of the opponents of socialism in the West is, not of course, the reduction of socialism to Gulag, in the style of 'new' French philosophers, but the information about the class structure of Western socities. There is an apparent decrease in the numbers of industrial workers, the true subject of revolution in Marx's sense, and an increase in middle classes: employees in various services, in mass media, in administration, and the professions. The middle classes opting for socialism cannot but mean one thing: the crisis of the existing system is so deep that even those social classes who in the past followed policies of maximum stability and security now express their dissatisfaction with the mere preservation of the *status quo* and are taking the risk of social change.

Thus there are at least three reasons for a renewed interest in socialism: first, there is a profound crisis in all existing systems and official ideologies. A mere extrapolation of prevailing trends and patterns of behaviour leads to stagnation, decay and eventual collapse of present day civilisation. Democratic socialism may be a way out.

Second, in search of valuable guidance one has to bracket official political culture and re-examine counter-cultural trends, especially their basic critical ideas and underlying value commitments. Thus one has to dissociate socialism from Stalinism, and go back to its roots in the great utopian thinkers, in Marx and his creative followers, and in libertarian socialists.

Third, a radical social change is needed for humankind to

survive and continue to develop. However, only those changes may be characterised as radical that transform human relations – and this is precisely what socialism is about. A new interest in socialism will focus on the possibilities of the humanisation of work, politics, culture and other areas of social life.

Since the main purpose of this book is to spell out the full meaning of the idea of a democratic, libertarian socialism, it cannot deal extensively with the nature of the present day crisis, which opens up the historical possibility and the need for such a socialist alternative. It must suffice to indicate how it differs from all earlier crises of capitalism which were successfully resolved within the framework of the given system.

What has become problematic and indeed doomed in present day, bourgeois society is not one of the accidental features that can be sacrificed without loss of identity, such as unlimited competition, strict separation of the civil sphere from the political sphere of society, full freedom of private initiative, military and political control of colonies as a means of economic control. It was possible to give up all these and yet preserve the same basic bourgeois structure. What cannot be given up without radical restructuring is an exponential growth of the production of material goods and services, consequently an exponential increase of the level of material consumption. Without such growth, without making out of accumulation and consumption of commodities the basic criterion of good life, capitalism would be unthinkable.

The tacit presuppositions of such an exponential growth were cheap labour; unlimited abundance of natural resources, and easy access to them; unrestrained pollution of the natural environment; unlimited possibilities of manipulation of the markets. All these presuppositions have diminished.

In the beginnings of capitalism, labour was even cheaper than in feudal times, but trade unions and labour political organisations were able to reverse that trend. More recently, natural resources have become increasingly expensive and have been considerably depleted within the last few decades. Even where they are still abundant they require expensive technology to be used, and are no longer easily accessible following the collapse of colonial empires at the end of the

Second World War. The capitalist West now faces an awakened, resistant Third World that dominates world political organisation, defies military threats and is a hard bargainer on the world markets.

Industrial production has polluted the air, waters and earth to such alarming proportions that the limit becomes conceivable beyond which the destruction of life on earth would be total and irreversible. Growing ecological consciousness does not only make further production costlier, it clashes with its very basic premise: indiscriminate production for profit rather than careful selective production for genuine human needs.

The very ability to distinguish between genuine and artificial human needs expresses a spirit that is sharply critical of mindless exponential growth. A steadily increasing material output requires large-scale production of needs which can subjectively be experienced as important, but, in fact, have nothing to do with real conditions of survival, development and self-fulfilment. Powerful, contemporary mass media are still able to manipulate the masses and turn them into docile, aping consumers. But the resistance to this sort of manipulation grows steadily out of necessity, if not out of wisdom: one returns to sanity when madness begins to look suicidal.

When the costs of production become too high, domestic resources depleted and consumers resistant to manipulation, when foreign markets shrink, former colonies turn into exploiters and new colonial wars become unprofitable and self-destructive, capitalism reaches a point when its own middle classes begin to look for an alternative.

Democratic socialism constitutes an optimal alternative for a vast majority of people. It continues to develop knowledge and to increase human productive powers. However those powers would be used for rational purposes such as satisfaction of basic needs of all people; decrease of working hours; preservation of a healthy natural environment; investments into humanisation of work and into culture. Higher productivity and higher standards of living could go together with less mechanical work and a stationary material output. Obviously this is possible only if the very concept of the standard of living changes its meaning. It would not be determined in terms of the *quantity* of consumed goods, but in terms of the *quality* of various life-manifestations, of the richness of needs generated and satisfied, of the meaningfulness of activities undertaken. Such a change involves a change in the attitude to nature. Ongoing development of knowledge and technology allows an increasing control over blind natural forces, however, in the absence of a rush for profits, a drive to conquer and ravage nature would be replaced by a concern to stay always in harmony with nature, and to use wisely its potential for human purposes.

In the same way in which conquering and ravaging nature invites a drive to dominate and plunder, harmony with nature goes together with a tendency to harmonise relations with other people. The basic philosophical principle in the former case is *dominating* power, in the latter case it is *creative* power. Domination leads inevitably to conflict: one can be a master only if someone is turned into a slave. Creativity, on the other hand, is not exclusive, involves compatibility, can be – even needs to be – shared.

From the distinction between dominating and creative power it does not follow that democratic socialism is a form of society in which everybody is creative. No form of society can guarantee anything in personal lives: it can only set up an institutional framework for such social relations which would facilitate or aggravate individual development and creativity. Democratic socialism tends to eliminate any form of domination, any monopoly of economic or political power; thus it opens a space in which each individual has a chance to realise fully his creative capacities.

This kind of social philosophy may be the only one which allows humankind to avoid the two pitfalls of ecological catastrophe and nuclear holocaust.

In what follows, *Part One* will deal with the basic humanist principles of this philosophy, and with a theory of social change that examines the historical conditions of its implementation.

*Part Two* is a systematic discussion of crucial social issues of work, State, law, political institutions, culture and morality. The purpose here is not to offer a blueprint for a perfect society, but to indicate what seem to be the optimal solutions of our present day problems.

After all the surprising experiences with socialist movements in this century, we may be wiser than our predecessors. But we do not yet know how great are our own illusions, and how many other possibilities there are that we cannot yet even dream about.

Belgrade, 20 June 1981

# PART I:

## *THEORY OF RADICAL SOCIAL CHANGE*

# I Basic Characteristics of Marxist Humanism

The growth of humanist theories and movements has usually been a symptom of an increased readiness to resist various alienated social forces such as Church, market, State, ideology, and technology. Great humanist philosophers and writers have invariably expressed revolt against these social structures in which man has been degraded or belittled. The recent universal surge of humanist literature can be accounted for only by the deeply-rooted anxieties of a generation which had to survive not only Nazi atrocities but also the Stalinist purges, and now the brutal slaughtering in South-East Asia, Latin America and Afghanistan.

And still 'humanism' is one of the most ambiguous and most misused of terms. Even those who have never shown in practice any real concern for human freedom and dignity sometimes like to play one of those humanist verbal games which are so easy to learn and even easier to repeat.

A natural reaction to this is a desire to dismiss the very notion of humanism. For example, Herbert Marcuse, in his paper at the Korčula Summer School in August 1968, expressed the view that humanism in general, including socialist humanism, is obsolete and that it belongs to the culture of a society which has already been overcome. He continued by expounding a plea for a new type of man, with new needs, values, and aspirations. This plea was clearly nothing else but a demand for a humanist qualitative change.

## 1 Limitations of liberal humanism

If misleading concepts and misuses cannot and need not be fought by dismissing important and well-entrenched terms, some necessary distinctions must be made. One is the distinction between *descriptive* and *normative* concepts of humanism. The former refers to common features of various historically

Descriptive

given forms of humanism. Humanism, in this sense, can be defined as a general concern for man while approaching all theoretical or practical problems. This means rejection of any transcendental and supernatural conception of the world. Our picture of the universe is contingent upon our sensory powers, language, capacities of thinking and imagination, and instruments and habits of our practical activity. Our theory of knowledge and logic depends on the historically given level of the human conceptual apparatus and accumulated experience. All values are relative to human needs, feelings, and preferences. The meaning of human life and striving is created by man himself. Many philosophical trends are humanistic in this sense, even those which do not have any explicit theory of man and do not pay much attention to anthropological, ethical, aesthetic, and political problems. Such is, for example, the 'humanism' of Ferdinand Cunning Scot Shiller (1864–1937) who, in opposition to abstract and depersonalised formal logic, elaborated a theory of knowledge and logic relative to practical experience and existing human language.

Humanism as a *normative* concept is a projection of a possible ideal future of man and of society. It is the expression of some specific values and, at least implicitly, a programme of practical action. Humanism in this sense varies from one trend to another: it has a definite meaning just in so far as it challenges or even excludes all other humanistic philosophies. That is why some Marxists three decades ago made considerable efforts to show that existentialism was not humanism. That is why there are always some bourgeois philosophers who try to show the lack of humanism in Marxism.

Marxism itself is a whole cluster of opposing orientations and tendencies, some of which can hardly be classified as humanism in any sense. And although all these various orientations clash with 'liberal humanism', the reasons for disagreement are vastly different.

Some contemporary forms of Marxism disregard the problem of individual freedom because they are ideologies of backward or fairly developed, but bureaucratic societies. In the former case, the whole society still faces the tasks of the capitalist epoch; accelerated industrialisation and urbanisation require centralised methods, and considerable sacrifices from individuals; the general level of education and culture is still low. Under such conditions there can be no question of superseding 'liberal humanism'. In the latter case, society remains below the level of already historically possible individual freedom. Disregard for personal freedom is, in both cases, the consequence of internal weaknesses of such societies.

However, those variants of Marxism which follow Marx in projecting the possibilities of an already developed industrialised and democratic society are opposed to the classical bourgeois liberal humanism from an entirely different point of view: the problem is not to proclaim the principle of individual freedom and full personal development in an abstract, purely theoretical, ahistorical, acritical way. The problem is how to realise this principle in practice? In which concrete form can it be materialised under existing historical conditions? Which existing social structures and institutions must be abolished in order to make room for a freer and richer life for all individuals?

Individual freedom in the *economic* sphere in every society based on commodity production requires unlimited private initiative and consequently growing social differentiation. Herbert Spencer merely drew all the logical consequences from this *laissez-faire* conception when he condemned all governmental intervention. Poverty, according to him, is a natural result of inefficiency, stupidity, and weakness of character. Therefore intervention in favour of the poor is unfair because it negates the fundamental law of equal freedom. In addition, State intervention is always in the interest of one particular group and against the interest of other groups. This is true: State intervention in the conditions of the market economy leads inevitably to bureaucratisation. Thus, liberal humanism has to choose between the inhumanity of *laissez-faire* capitalism and the anti-liberal bureaucracy of State capitalism. Or perhaps something should be done about the assumption of commodity production? But what? And how, within the framework of liberal humanism?

Intellectual freedom is 'freedom of thought and inquiry', 'freedom of speech and publication', 'the freedom to teach, preach and advocate', etc. Other conditions being equal, the very proclamation of these freedoms constitutes an enormous achievement in the process of human emancipation. But other conditions are not equal. Funds for scientific research are alienated from the research worker. The mass media of communication are either possessed or fully controlled by those who have nothing to say, and especially nothing new nor heretical. And the vast majority of mankind, anyway, has not the slightest chance to enjoy any intellectual activities, free or unfree.

Political freedoms – the 'right of opposition, election, petition, recall, the right of assembly' – really are *conditio sine qua non* of every democratic society. However, the mere proclamation of these freedoms in practice means little in every society in which there are one or more political parties with their bureaucratic party machines, enormous funds, and developed techniques for the manipulation of individuals.

Self-management and various forms of participation of individuals in social communities in which they live and work, might, under certain conditions, be a decisive step towards abolition of alienated labour. To be sure, participation in a private enterprise is at best, a palliative measure. Selfmanagement within scattered, atomised, disintegrated enterprises, still subordinated to bureaucratic structures at the level of the global society, must be taken as only the first important step in the process of workers' emancipation. If this first step is not followed by further ones, if the permanently developing, integrating system of self-management does not gradually replace the organs of the State and professional politics, the principle itself might be compromised and reduced to one more of the sweet nothings of contemporary social life.

The difference between traditional liberal humanism and the democratic contemporary form of Marx's humanism does not consist, therefore, in the fact that the former is concerned primarily with the human *individual* and the latter with the totality of *social* phenomena. The real issue is whether radical individual emancipation is feasible without radical change of the whole social structure: and how, and in what sense, it would be possible for an individual to be really freer, more capable of expressing all his potential powers, of developing a need for satisfying the needs of other members of his community, if he continued to produce commodities for the market; if political power remained alienated, embodied in the State and political parties; if a monopoly of the mass media survived; and if factories of *ersatz* culture continued their production of ever cheaper and increasingly more worthless magazines, television programmes, comic books, etc.

The real issue, therefore, is whether humanism remains *pure theory*, satisfied with verbal declarations and abolition of existing alienation *in thought*, or is a theory which immediately implies a programme of *practical* dis-alienation.

## 2   The specific nature of a humanism of praxis

Marxism is essentially a humanism of *praxis*, a philosophy which tends towards as complete a unification of theory and practical action as possible. This unity affects both theory and practice. Theory assumes the role of a permanently vivid and concrete critical self-consciousness and thus becomes a major historical force. Practice becomes enlightened both by a global vision of an ideally possible future, and by a critical understanding of the existing historical situation and its inherent possibilities for change. Thus Marxist humanism is opposed to all those trends which see the meaning of philosophy in the analysis of positive knowledge, in passive wisdom, in understanding and explanation which lead only to adjustment or to powerless intellectual revolt. In particular, it is opposed to a pragmatic, existentialist, and Stalinistic conception of human practice.

*Pragmatism* lacks a universal, humanistic vision: it also neglects the role of prior theory. Man, as presupposed by pragmatism, is an atomised, isolated individual with his particular interest; an individual who has not yet become a social being, who remains enclosed within the boundaries of his given and reified world. This activity is irrational and utilitarian.

Human activity also remains irrational within the framework of *existentialist* philosophy. If man has no definite structure to his being, which is the product of all previous history, a structure which thus precedes any act of choice and engagement and determines the limits of the possible, then everything is equally possible and no theoretical knowledge about the past can be relevant for the future. Our activity is, therefore, purely voluntaristic. Only *a posteriori* shall we know whether the goals have been really possible, and only then will our activity acquire a definite meaning.

This view is not without merit as the expression of revolt against the conformism of the majority of intellectuals who merely adapt to what is given and to what prevails. Existentialist humanism rejects this rationality of 'great numbers' which avoids any radical change or risk – which loyally serves the existing social order.

An existentialist in action refuses to be burdened by knowledge, refuses to be realistic and wise, because uncritical knowledge and conformistic wisdom lead only to inessential improvements and reforms, never to radical transformations. By refusing to admit any boundaries, any conditioning by the past, he achieves a good deal of freshness and spontaneity of behaviour, he acquires the possibility of creating something really new on the margin between the possible and impossible. But this novelty can only arise by chance. An enormous number of such blind choices and a tremendous waste of human energy are needed to create something really new and really important in this way. Such activity of atomised individuals, if transferred from the fields of poetry, of the arts and play to politics, again leads to the rule of 'the law of great numbers'. Various unco-ordinated individual actions cancel each other and the historical process remains determined by unknown blind forces. All spontaneity and originality of behaviour of isolated, authentic personalities remain only a hardly observable embellishment on the margin of great, impersonal, historical streams of events. These streams can be modified and redirected only by co-ordinate activity of large social collectives which are engaged in order to materialise a real, even if not very probable, possibility.

The Marxist approach to the problem of the praxis of an individual is superior to existenialism in at least two respects. First, it eliminates the utterly simplified view that all knowledge is a source of conformism. Critical knowledge, as distinguished from positive or technical knowledge, provides information about negative, destructive forces within a system (e.g. Marx's law of decreasing rate of profit in capitalism). Thus it allows the discovery of hidden real possibilities of radical change. Second, while existentialism overestimates the possibilities of spontaneous individual actions, Marxism realises that an individual can decisively influence the course of history only in so far as he succeeds in expressing and articulating the real needs of a whole social group to which he belongs.

With respect to both these points an ideological mystification typical of bureaucratic abuse of Marxism must be avoided. Bureaucracy also proclaims a readiness to change the world and, as positive science does not suffice for that purpose, it wants to supplement it by a 'revolutionary theory'. On the other hand, bureaucracy keeps repeating that only the broad masses, especially the workers, can make history.

However, by 'the change of the world' bureaucracy does not mean a real supersession of existing forms of alienation, including institutions of professional politics, but only small improvements and reforms. 'Revolutionary theory' tends to be as militant and uncompromising as possible only with respect to the external capitalist world; with respect to the initial forms of socialism it is utterly conservative and apologetic. Bureaucracy still tries to play the role of the workers' *avant-garde* but instead of expressing the real needs and interests of workers, it expects the workers to follow loyally all the twists and turns of its policy. But if workers ever rebel they are labelled 'mob', 'subversive', or 'the weapon of the class enemy'. The rule of bureaucracy rests on a double basis: sheer brute force, and, an ideology which tries to rationalise its policy and its social position.

The rationality implicit in Marxist humanism is fundamentally different from both *ideological* rationality and from the rationality of *positive* science.

For ideological rationality an effort is characteristic to express the interests and needs of a particular social group in the form of mutually linked, systematised, indicative statements whose main function is to mystify real social relationships and to create the appearance of a universally valid *Weltanschauung*. In order to de-mystify this kind of apparent rationality it is necessary to show not only that seemingly factual statements are often only value judgements in disguise, but also that these value judgements express not universal but particular interests and needs.

For the rationality of positive science, on the contrary, a characteristic tendency is to exclude all value judgements as irrational. However, in this way the question about the fundamental goals of human activity is removed to a sphere of irrationality. Rationality is thus reduced to the rationality of means, and consequently to technological rationality. No matter how irrational and inhuman are the goals, maximum efficiency in the process of their realisation would also signify the maximum of rationality. And this best shows the absurd character of such a limited concept of rationality.

The Marxist notion of rationality includes both fact and value, knowledge and ideal. But in contrast to positivism, the idea of an integral, critical knowledge is assumed by Marxism. It is differentiated from any ideological axiology, which projects the interests of a particular social group into an ahistorical, transcendental sphere of being; Marxist rationality presupposes a universal ideal of possible emancipation, solidarity, and fulfilment in a concrete historical form.

The concepts of science and theory have a fundamentally new meaning in Marxist humanism. This is the consequence not only of an ever present practical orientation, but also of the application of a new method of thought: dialectics.

Scientific theory which one finds in *Capital* is neither empirical in the ordinary sense, nor purely speculative. It is not a mere description and explanation of actually given phenomena but a study of possibilities. This study is based on ample empirical evidence. Thus the possibilities in question are projections within a real historical situation. However, the projections are strongly coloured by a philosophical vision. The starting point of inquiry is not just a mass of empirical data but an elaborated, anthropological theory and a critical examination of all relevant previous theoretical knowledge.

The essential part of building up a new theory is the creation of a new conceptual apparatus. These concepts have both explanatory and critical functions. Dialectics is essentially a method of criticism, of discovery of inner limitations, tensions, and conflicts. Contemporary *historicism*, which is primarily interested in diachronic aspects of social formations, and *structuralism*, which pays attention only to synchronic aspects, are only partial moments of Marx's method. According to this method, scientific theory tends to examine whole structures – totalities, not isolated events. But a structure becomes meaningful only when it is conceived as a crystallisation of the past forms of human practice, and with respect to historically possible futures. On the other hand, what is historically possible can be established only by taking into account the structural characteristics of the whole situation. To be sure structural characteristics are constituted not solely by the static factors which preserve the stability of the system, but also by dynamic factors which lead to dysfunction and destruction.

Thus the role of science is not only to provide positive knowledge and to secure maximum efficiency within the framework of a given social system, it also discovers other possibilities of the system which correspond better to human needs. Thus critical science shows not only how man can best adjust to the dominating historical tendencies within a given social framework, but also how he can change the whole framework and adjust it to himself.

## 3   The idea of praxis

This entire analysis rests on a concept of human nature that penetrates beneath a vast variety of manifested, observable features of human behaviour in history and reveals a permanent potential capacity of man to act in an imaginative, creative way, to produce ever new objects and forms of social life, and so change not only his environment but to evolve himself. Man is often inert and passive; he occasionally manifests a strong irrational drive to destroy; and, in general, he has many conflicting latent dispositions (to be independent and free, but also to escape responsibility; to belong to a social community, but also to pursue selfish private goals; to live in peace and security, but also to compete and be aggressive). These latent dispositions are empirically testable in the sense that they can be brought to life and observed when appropriate conditions are created. Some of them have been responsible for the great achievements in human history, and are worthy of being reinforced; others have led to great disasters or long periods of decay and stagnation and should be modified or overcome.

The capacity for praxis is taken to be the essential characteristic of man precisely because it was and remains the necessary and sufficient condition of human history. In all real historical moments, moments of novelty, individuals and whole large collectives acted in a specifically human way which distinguished them from the behaviour of animals in the following respects:

1 Specifically human activity, praxis involves a conscious, purposeful change of objects. This change is not repetitious, it introduces novelty. Man rebels against any form of limitation, be it from the external world or from within himself. Novelty is essentially the overcoming of limitation.

2 Praxis is the objectification of all the wealth of specifically human potential capacities and powers. It is an activity which is a goal in itself and free in the positive sense of genuine self-realisation. Therefore it is profoundly pleasurable for its own sake, no matter how much effort and energy it might require.

3 While it involves self-affirmation, praxis also mediates between one individual and another, and establishes a *social relation* between them. In the process of praxis an individual is immediately aware that through his activity and his product he satisfies the needs of other individuls, enriches their life, and indirectly becomes part of them. Thus through praxis an individual becomes a *social being*.

4 Finally, praxis is *universal*, in the sense that by continual learning man is able to incorporate in his activity the modes of action and production of all other living beings and all other nations and civilisations.

These potential characteristics of a specifically human, free and creative activity very rarely come to expression under the conditions of modern industrial production and modern political life.

## 4  Alienated labour

The work of the vast majority of human beings, owing to a series of historical conditions, does not have a specifically human character and may be described as a tremendous waste of human potential – as *alienated labour*.

When the necessity for an increase in the productivity of labour results in the division of labour, in the partition of society into professional groups, in the polarisation of manual and intellectual workers and of managers and employees, in the crumbling and atomising of the entire working process into individual phases, and finally in setting-up operations around which the whole life of the individual or groups of workers may sometimes be fixed, the entire structure of human work disintegrates and an acute gap between its constituent elements appears: the product no longer has its determined producer, and the producer loses all connection with the object produced.

This is a two-sided externalisation (*Entäusserung*) for the product not only escapes from the control of its creator, but it also begins to act like an independent power which treats its maker like an object, like a thing to be used.[1] This phenomenon is possible because behind the object there is another man who uses it to transform the producer into a thing, where human qualities are completely irrelevant except for one: this is a special kind of commodity which can produce other commodities and which needs for its upkeep and reproduction a smaller amount of objectified work (in the form of wages) than the amount of objectified work (the value of the product) which it creates. This two-sided externalisation, which in essence is not a relation of a man to the natural object, but rather a specific relationship of a man toward other man, is *alienation*.[2]

Marx did not discover the concept of alienated labour; it can be found in Hegel's early work. However, Marx reopened a problem which Hegel had fictively solved and closed. He gave it a real historical perspective within the framework of a general humanistic philosophical vision. While working on *Grundrisse der Kritik der politischen Oekonomie* and in his first draft of *Capital*, Marx rarely used the term 'alienation' itself, but the conceptual structure expressed therein was the basis for his entire critique of political economy.

Marx's critical position in *Capital* can only be understood in the light of his hypothesis of true human community and true production where each man both 'affirms himself and the other man'.

The analysis of labour in *Capital* is the starting point for the explanation and criticism of capitalist society, and of any other society which is based on commodity production. The character of labour is contradictory. A part of what Marx, in his earlier works called 'alienated labour', is now placed under the term 'abstract labour'. Only abstract labour creates exchange value, and only it has a socially acknowledged importance. However, man's labour is here totally crippled, deprived of everything personal, free, creative, spontaneous, or human, and reduced to being a simple supplement to machines. The only socially acknowledged characteristic of that labour will be its quantity, and this will be judged on the market and will receive its abstract objective form – money. The fetishism of commodities, the mysticism of the merchandise world, are the concepts by which, within the sphere of economics, Marx expressed the same structure of productive relations which he termed in his earlier works 'alienated labour'. Again, the point is, as Marx says in *Capital*, that 'their [the commodity producer's], own historical movement takes the form of the movement of things under whose control they happen to be placed, instead of having control over them'.[3] The conclusion which Marx draws from his analyses of the production of relative surplus value reproduces, in condensed form, all the elements of his criticism of alienated labour in early writings:

> Within the capitalist system all methods for increasing social productive forces are carried out at the expense of the individual worker, all means for developing production degenerate into means for the exploitation of and rule over the producer. They make a cripple out of the worker, a semi-man; they reduce him to the common equipment of a machine, destroy the last remains of appeal in his work transforming it into a real torture. They alienate from the worker the intellectual possibilities of the process of labour to the degree in which science is included as an independent force. They deform the conditions under which he works, subject him in the process of labour to a disgusting and pedantic despotism, transform his entire life into working hours and throw his wife and his child under the juggernaut's wheel of capital.[4]

In his *Economic and Philosophical Manuscripts*,[5] Marx distinguished four types of alienation of the worker:
1 alienation from the product of labour, which becomes an independent blind power;
2 alienation from the production itself, which becomes compulsive and routine and loses any traits of creativity (which, among other things, implies production according to the laws of beauty);
3 alienation from the human generic being, for whom conscious, free and productive labour is characteristic;
4 alienation from the other man, because satisfaction of another's needs, supplementing another's being, cease to be the prime motive of production.
All of these aspects of alienation can be found in *Capital*.

The fetish character of commodities lies precisely in the fact that 'the social characteristics of their own work seem to people to be characteristics which objectively belong to the products of labour themselves, to be properties which those things have by nature'. Hence, 'social relationships among people assume for them a phantasmagorical form of the relationships among things'. *making into an object*

This reification of human relations springs from specific characteristics of labour which produces commodities. Labour can take on the character of a commodity only 'when various specific cases of work are reduced to a common character which they all have as the expenditure of working capacity, as human labour in the abstract'. This abstract labour ceases to be a need and fulfilment of the human being and becomes the mere necessary means of its subsistence. 'The accumulation of wealth at one end is at the same time the accumulation of poverty, hard labour, slavery, ignorance, growing bestiality, and moral decline at the other, that is, on the part of the class which brings forth its own product in the shape of capital'.[6]

The alienation of the producer from the other man stems from the simple fact that the purpose of the work is no longer the satisfaction of another's needs, but rather the possibility of transforming labour into money – the general and impersonal form of objectified labour. Extreme forms of alienation among people arise as a consequence of the competition, exploitation, and despotism to which the worker is subjected. In order to increase production, and at the same time to prevent a decline in the profit rate, it becomes necessary to squeeze out from the worker an increasingly large amount of unpaid work.[7] Hence, the necessity for the most efficient manipulation of workers possible, and the need for an increase in the degree of the exploitation of labour.

Criticism of alienated labour, therefore, is present in both *Capital* and in all earlier works. One who loses sight of this criticism also loses the possibility of understanding the deepest meaning of Marx's message, and opens himself up to the dangerous illusion that many historical problems have already been resolved when all that have been realised are some preconditions and all that have been achieved are some first steps towards their resolution.

Marx carefully explained in his earlier writings that *private property is not the cause but the consequence of alienated labour*, just as gods are originally the consequence not the cause of religious alienation. Only later does conditioning become reciprocal. In the society which Marx calls 'primitive', 'non-reflective communism', 'man's personality is negated in every sphere', the entire world of culture and civilisation regresses towards the unnatural simplicity of the poor and wantless individual, who has not only not surpassed private property, but has not yet even attained to it.[8] In this kind of society, Marx says, 'the community is only a community of *work* and of *equality of wages* paid with communal capital by the community as universal capitalist'.[9]

That is why Marx felt that the basic question was that of the *nature of labour* rather than the question of private property. 'In speaking of private property, one believes oneself to be dealing with something external to mankind. But in speaking of labour one deals directly with mankind itself. This new formulation of the problem already contains its solution.'[10]

The solution, therefore, is to abolish those relations into which the worker comes during the process of his labour, to abolish the situation in which he becomes only one of the commodities in the reified world of commodities. The essence of exploitation lies in the fact that accumulated, objectified labour – that is, capital – rules over live work and appropriates the value which it creates, which is greater than the value of the labour force itself. Marx expressed this major thesis in *Capital*, in the following concise manner: 'The rule of capital over the worker is merely the rule of things over man, of dead over live labour'.[11]

The specific historical form which enabled the appropriation of objectified labour in Marx's time was the disposal of capital on the basis of private ownership of the means of production. This specific feature clouded over the generality of its content and it is no wonder that to many Marxists it seemed, and still seems, that the existence of exploitation in a society in which private enterprises have been nationalised is a *contradictio in adjecto*. Nevertheless, it is obvious that private ownership of the means of production is not the only social institution which allows for the disposal of objectified labour. First, in a market economy during the transitional period, this institution can be the monopolistic position of individual collectives which enables them to sell their commodities above their value. Such collectives, in fact, appear on the market as collective capitalists and collective exploiters. (Needless to say, within the process of internal distribution this appropriated surplus of value will never reach the pockets of the producers themselves, but rather will find its way into the bureaucratic and technocratic elements of the enterprise.) Second, it can be a monopoly over the decision-making in a Statist system. To the degree to which a bureaucracy exists and takes control of objectified labour into its own hands, rewarding itself with various privileges, there is no doubt that this is only another form of appropriating the surplus value created by the working class.

The only way definitely to abolish exploitation is to create the conditions which will prevent objectified labour from ruling over live labour, in which, above all, the right to *dispose of objectified labour will be given to the producers themselves.*

## 5  Political alienation

Alienation in the field of material production entails a corresponding form of alienation in the field of public, social life, the State, and politics: politics are separated from economics, and society is divided into two opposite spheres. One is *civil society* with all the egoism of the concrete owner of commodities, with all its envy, greed for private possession and indifference towards the true needs of others. The other sphere is that of the *political society* of the abstract citizen which, in an illusory way, personifies within itself the general interest of the community.

Kant and Hegel outlined two basic but contrary concepts of the State and law. Kant's liberal concept starts from the real, empirically given society, characterised by the market and the mutual competition among egotistic individuals, and attempts to reconcile the general interest and freedom of the individual in a negative manner by demanding restriction of the self-initiative and arbitrariness of the individual. Hegel correctly perceived that simple common co-existence and mutual restriction of selfish individuals do not constitute a true human community. He, therefore, tried to transcend this negative relationship of one individual with the next, seen as his limit, by the assumption of a *rational citizen* and a *rational community* in which the individual relates positively to the social whole, and through it to other individuals. However, Hegel himself remained within the framework of the limited horizon of bourgeois society, conceiving rationality as an abstract iden- tification of the subjective spirit of the individual with the objective spirit of the State. The State as the personification of ideal human community is a pure abstraction which fictively transcends the existing empirical reality of bourgeois society.

In his criticism of Hegel's philosophy of law, Marx properly observed that a) such a reduction of a concrete possible human community to an abstraction of the State (the moment of the objective spirit), along with reducing a concrete, historically given individual to an abstraction of the citizen, takes the form of alienation; and that b) this alienation in thought is the result of alienation in the reality itself. The picture of the modern State imagined by the Germans, was possible only because the State abstracts itself from true people and fulfils the total man in only an imaginary way.[12]

Contrary to civil society, in which there is *bellum omnium contra omnes*, and in which only intersecting and mutually contradictory separate interests come to expression, in the political society the State-in-general appears as a necessary sup- plement, and in Hegel's conception it 'exists *an sich* and *für sich*'. The State, then, is an alienated universal and necessarily entails the formalism of the State – namely bureaucracy. Bureaucracy attempts to affirm general interest as something special, *beside and above all other private and special interests*.[13] In this way it presents itself as an alienated social power which treats the world as a mere object of its activity.[14] On the other hand, the State and bureaucracy are necessary supplements to the crumbling world of the owners of commodities, who all follow only their special and private goals. The State also supports a special interest but creates the illusion of its general- ity. 'General interest can be maintained in face of special inter- est only as something "particular" inasmuch as the particular in fact of the general is maintained as something general.'[15]

Needless to say, this dualism between the bureaucratised State and special private interests was impossible to resolve by identifying these contradictions in an imaginary way, within the framework of abstract thought.

'The abolition of bureaucracy,' says Marx, 'is possible only when general interest becomes *reality*,' and when 'special interest really becomes *general* interest.'[15] And that is only possible when the individual man begins to live, work, and relate to his fellow man in a human way 'only when man ceases to separate his *forces propres* as a social power from himself in the form of political power, only then will human emancipation be achieved.'[17]

Marx explained this conception more clearly in *Grundrisse*. Here he compares political with religious alienation; in both cases man projects his general, human, generic characteristics and needs either onto an out-of-this-world being, or onto the State. Both are a necessary supplement to the incomplete social reality and can wither away only when man liberates himself from the idiocy of tying his entire life to one calling or to wage labour.

Marx shows in *Capital* that all the basic rights guaranteed by the State to its citizens have a formal and alienated character. Freedom is merely the citizen's right to dispose of his commodity. Equality is in reality merely the application of the principle of equality to the exchange of commodity.[18] Everyone looks out for himself and not for the other. General good can only be realised 'behind the back of the individual' by the 'invisible hand', as Adam Smith says. For Marx, the question is how to strive for the general goals of the community consciously and freely, and in the most rational and most human way possible. For that, the State is no longer necessary. 'Freedom consists in transforming the State from an organ which dominates society into an organ which is completely subordinate to it, and even at the present, the forms of the State are more or less free to the degree that they limit the freedom of the State.'[19]

## 6  Emancipation and self-government

In his early work *The Poverty of Philosophy*, Marx offered the theory that 'in the process of its development the working class will replace the old civil society with an association which excludes classes and their contradictions. Then there will no

longer be political rule in the traditional sense, because political rule is precisely the official expression for the class contradictions in civil society.'[20] In the *Communist Manifesto* Marx says
that achieving democracy is the first step in the workers'
revolution. The new State will be nothing more than 'the
proletariat organised as the ruling class'.[21] Marx's conception
of the fate of the State during the revolution is particularly
clear in his analysis of the experiences of the Paris Commune.
He talks throughout of 'destroying State rule', of 'smashing'
it, of its being 'superfluous'. With enthusiasm he accepts two
'infallible means', (as Engels calls them), for preventing
bureaucratism. First, 'the Commune appointed for its officials
persons elected by the general vote, persons who are directly
responsible and at any time replaceable by their electors'.
Second, 'public office, whether it concerns high or low positions, had to be performed for workers' wages'.[22] For the first
time in history, if only for a short period, the State was
replaced by self-management.

In his *Paris Manuscripts* of 1844, the road to overcoming
alienated labour was not yet clear to Marx. He makes only a
rough draft here of the general vision of a society in which all
individuals develop freely, and realise themselves as complete
personalities. Social relationships are no longer those of envy,
competition, abuse, or mutual indifference, but rather relations in which the individual, while fulfilling the needs of the
next man, while enrichening the being of other persons,
directly experiences his own affirmation and self-realisation as
a man.

Marx gives a concrete historical dimension to this general
vision of transcending alienated labour in his *Grundrisse*. It was
entirely clear to Marx that new, more human relations of
production will occur only in an advanced society, in the
production relations which, thanks to the scientific and technological progress, have already become universal, no matter
how reified. Only when man is no longer directly governed by
people but by abstract forces, by reified social laws, will the
possibility be created to bring these reified conditions of existence under communal social control.

In *Capital*, Marx's solution for the problem of alienation of
labour is quite clearly outlined, for example, in the discussion
on the fetishism of commodities. 'The form of the process of

social life, i.e. of the process of material production will cast off from itself the mystical, foggy veil only when the product of freely associated people is under their conscious, planned control. But this requires such a material basis and such a set of material conditions which in themselves are the wild product of a long and painful history of development'.[23] One should particularly underline the famous passage in the third volume of *Capital* where Marx says:

> Freedom in the field of material production cannot consist of anything else but the fact that socialised man, associated producers, regulate their interchange with nature rationally, bring it under their common control, instead of being ruled by it as by some blind power; that they accomplish their task with the least expenditure of energy and under conditions most adequate to their human nature and most worthy of it.[24]

All basic elements of self-management are already given here:

1 The regulation of the process of labour should be left in the hands of the workers themselves; it cannot remain the monopoly of any special profession of managers who concern themselves with that only, and who, as the only historical subjects, will manipulate all other people like objects.

2 Producers must be associated, and that association must be free. Self-management is not, therefore, a synonym for the atomisation and disintegration of society, as some of its opponents like to represent it and as it may appear in practice when mistakenly understood. Self-management assumes integration and this integration must be free and voluntary.

3 The control of production carried out by the associated producers must be conscious and planned; the exchange with nature must be regulated in a rational manner, and not abandoned to the rule of blind powers. Self-management, therefore, assumes constant direction, the elimination of uncontrolled economic forces. That presupposes the development of culture and science, and a clear understanding of the goals of development.

4 This communal control and direction of material production should engage as little human energy as possible, for managing things – and above all people – cannot be a goal in itself, but only a means for securing truly free, creative, and spontaneous activity.

5 The kind of self-management which Marx had in mind is

possible only with a relatively high degree of social develop-ment. According to him, it 'requires the kind of material basis which is the result of the long and painful history of develop-ment'. However, if something is ever to achieve a developed form, it must start to develop in time. That is why Marx investigated so seriously and with such interest the experience of the Paris Commune and derived conclusions from it for the practice of the workers' movement. That is why history will certainly justify the efforts in Yugoslavia to begin with the introduction of the first, initial forms of self-management even if in unripe conditions.

6 Still, in observing the conditions under which the exchange with nature is to take place, Marx does not consider the greatest success and efficiency, the greatest increase in power over nature, the greatest material wealth as the most important things. For him, it is of greatest importance to carry out this process under those conditions which are the *most adequate and the most worthy of the human nature of the worker.*

Marx concludes the third volume of *Capital* with the same humanist ideas which he expounded in *Economic and Philosophical Manuscripts* and other early writings.

## Notes

1 'Die Entäusserung des Arbeiters in seinem Product hat die Bedeutung nicht nur dass seine Arbeit zu einem Gegenstand, zu seiner ausseren Existenz wird sondern dass sie ausser ihn unabhängig, frei von ihm existiert und eine selbst-ständige Macht ihm gegenüber wird.' Marx and Engels, *Historisch-kritische Gesamtansgabe*, (Berlin: Marx-Engels Institut, 1932), vol. 3, p. 83.

2 'Durch die wechselseitige Entäusserung oder Entfremdung des Privateigentums, ist das Privateigentum selbst in die Bestimmung des Entäusserung Privateigun-tums geraten.' (Marx in MEGA, vol. 1, 3, p. 538.)

3 Marx, *Das Kapital*, (In Marx and Engels, *Werke*, Berlin, 1961), vol. 1, ch. 1, p. 4.

4 *Ibid*, vol. 1, ch. 23, p. 674.

5 See Marx, 'Alienated Labour', in Erich Fromm *Marx's Concept of Man*, pp. 93–103; also in Easton & Goudat *Writings of the Young Marx*, pp. 287–96.

6 Marx, *Das Kapital*, vol. 1, ch. 23, p. 675.

7 *Ibid*, vol. 3, ch. 14, sec. 1.

8 Marx, *Economic and Philosophical Manuscripts*, in Fromm, *Marx's Concept of Man*, p. 108.

9 *Ibid*, p. 125.

10 Ibid, p. 126.

11 *Marx-Engels Archiv* (Moscow 1933) p. 68.

12 Karl Marx, 'Kritik der Hegelschen Rechtsphilosophie', (*Werke*, vol. 1, p. 384–5).

13 In his 'Critique of Hegel's Philosophy of the State and of Law', Marx pointed out that in bureaucracy the identity of State interests and particular economic goals is

posed in such a way that State interest becomes a separate private goal competing with other private goals. (*Ibid*, p. 297.)

14 *Ibid*, p. 250.
15 *Ibid*, p. 248.
16 *Ibid*, p. 250.
17 Karl Marx, 'Zur Judenfrage', (MEGA, vol. 1, part 1, p. 599).
18 See Marx, *Das Kapital*, (Berlin 1947), vol. 1, p. 184.
19 'Kritik des Gothaer Programms' in Marx-Engels, *Werke*, vol. 19, p. 27.
20 Marx, *The Poverty of Philosophy*, MEGA, vol. 4, p. 182.
21 *The Communist Manifesto*, in *The Marx-Engels Reader*, R.C. Tucker ed. (New York 1975), p. 353.
22 Karl Marx, 'Address to the General Council of International Workers' Union concerning the Civil War in France', in Marx-Engels, *Werk*, vol. 17, p. 339.
23 Marx, *Das Kapital*, vol. 1, ch. 1, sec. 4.
24 *Ibid*, vol. 3, ch. 48, sec. 2.

# 2 The Idea of Self-Governing Socialism

Eight decades after the Paris Commune and Marx's analysis of its experiences, the socialist movement has revived the forgotten idea of self-government. It has thus retrieved its soul, its deeply human values, and its universal historical meaning just at the moment when it seemed that in the West its time had run out, and that all that was left was the practice and theory of a specific way of industrialising the underdeveloped countries. For not only does democratic Socialism and a society based on self-government mean the radical negation and, in its most extreme fulfilment, the radical humanisation of contemporary capitalism, but furthermore it is a necessary means for the further development of existing embryonic forms of post-capitalistic society.

But the rediscovery and decisive affirmation of the principle of self-government have met bitter resistance from many who regard themselves as followers of Marx and builders of socialism. Part of the explanation must be sought in the economic and social conditions of certain countries in which the socialist transformation of society has already begun. Real self-government presupposes the existence of a reasonable number of rational, socialised, and humane persons who understand the major aim of the social process, persons who are themselves alive to the relative interlinking of personal, group and general interests and who base their activities on ideals of general human significance. An undeveloped, predominantly rural society does not have enough of such people, and moreover does not have all the preconditions for producing them relatively rapidly. Thus it cannot avoid that phase in its development in which an élite – at best a genuinely revolutionary élite – through the maximum mobilisation of the masses, and using compulsion, creates all the necessary preconditions – i.e. industry, a working class, an intelligentsia, schooling and mass culture. In the absence of these preconditions, self-government can only come to mean general disintegration.

However, the critical question is: will this élite, when these preconditions are realised, find within itself the moral strength and consistency to pass voluntarily to the basic element of the socialist revolution? (i.e. to the realisation of self-government, and consequently the gradual setting aside of itself as a power élite.) This does not mean that it cannot permanently remain as an élite of the mind, if it has a powerful mind. Or will several decades of intense concentration of power in its hands so change its social nature that this élite will identify itself with socialism and will want to cling permanently to its political and material privileges, and will want to remain permanently not only the mind but the iron hand of the historic process?

Thus a political factor of resistance to self-government joins the economic and social one. This factor is the existence of a political structure for which a greater or lesser degree of *bureaucratisation and political alienation* is characteristic.

Yugoslavia may claim the historic credit of having reintroduced the idea of self-government and begun its practical realisation. However, while it constitutes the very backbone of official Yugoslav ideology, in practice it is effectively thwarted and checked by bureaucratic elements, and, what is more significant, it is still understood as an institution which exists in addition to the State: an institution which embraces only local organs of social power. This means that not only has self-government not yet been fully realised but also that its full meaning is not properly understood. To explain this meaning is to explain the philosophical and political assumptions of social self-government and above all the concepts of political alienation and bureaucracy.


## 1  Political alienation in socialism

Under *politics* in the widest sense of the word I understand all those human activities of decision-making and realisation whereby important, public, social processes are regulated and directed. Marx was right in regarding politics in class society as a sphere of alienation. As a partial sphere of social activity and consciousness, isolated from morality, science, and philosophy, very much conditioned by the particular position and interests of the class concerned, politics had become one of the forms of practice in which every individual permanently missed the real possibilities of an authentic, rich human life.

But what of politics after the abolition of the ruling class of capitalistic society? While the revolutionary process of abolishing the political and economic power of the bourgeoisie is going on, important changes are taking place. The State apparatus of the old society is being destroyed from its very foundation, civil parties disappear, politics gains great significance owing to the fact that economics and science, culture and art become the object of the revolutionary, centralised regulation and direction. In addition, and what is particularly important, very considerable sections of the people become politically active, and take part directly in the process of transformation of the old society; or at least there is a lively feeling that the course of events depends on their attitude.

But then, as time passes, following the successful revolutionary encounter with the one-time ruling class, an ever clearer tendency appears to concentrate the majority of decisions concerning all key social questions in the hands of a limited group of rulers. Indeed, they take decisions in the name of others, often with their consent, and not infrequently with their real or potential support. But as soon as such a sharp division has been completed into those who are permanently political *subjects* who make decisions and implement them, and those who are political *objects* and who are called on only to agree with the decisions made, and to behave in agreement with them, it is not difficult to discover all the essential forms of political alienation. They are:

1 Man loses control over political institutions – the State, the party etc. – institutions which he has created and which function in his name. Thence his feeling of power decreases: he is not part of the political process and has no influence on the course of events. Political occurrences, including those when his active participation is called for (as in the case of elections) lose their meaning, for there is no real choice and his vote has no real part to play. For this reason politics ceases to offer any really intellectual or emotional satisfaction: the point is reached where people begin to withdraw and become apathetic. In such a situation there is moral degradation and a lowering of the standard of political behaviour of those who still find it useful to engage in politics. Now often fear, worry, or

craving for success become the primary motives of political activity.

2 Man alienates himself in a bureaucratic society from other people, no matter whether he falls within the group of those who rule or of those who are ruled. In the first case, there develops within him an explicitly inhuman feeling for hierarchy, for social status. In choosing those with whom he wishes to have closer relationships, he is guided primarily not by *what a man is*, but *what position he has*. In the second case, the politically apathetic individual in a society in which all politics are decided by other people, and in which his own rise and fall to a very large extent depend on what he is thought of in powerful political institutions, will often be tempted to play various roles which do not suit him, suspecting that others do the same. In this atmosphere of mistrust, insincerity, artificiality, many potentially human and intimate relationships between people die before they can begin to develop. In the drastic circumstances of a bureaucratic society (e.g. in the time of Stalin) the individual had at times to hide his political opinions even from members of his own family.

3 In a bureaucratic society political activity ceases to be *creative* activity. Thus a man who involves himself in politics alienates himself from one of his essential needs and from one of the essential possibilities of a really human way of his existence. Discussion of things about which conclusions have been previously prepared, elections of candidates already decided on in advance, criticism which – most certainly – will not have the slightest effect and which is in fact only part of a clearly defined ritual, all this gives political activity a purely manifestational character, turns it into a routine and empty formalism. It is for this reason that nowhere are there so many clichés, so many stereotypes, nowhere so much spiritual emptiness and boredom as in the functioning of a bureaucratic political apparatus.

4 Finally, all these conditions often lead to a complete split between the way in which man exists politically and his authentic potential being. We find one form of this conflict in those who are aware of their degradation and who know that their opportunist or bureaucratic existence is far below the level of what they *can* be and of what they *should* be.

A second form of the loss of the true self is to be found in caesaristic political structures. The history of socialism will record that such structures often appeared in the initial bureaucratic phases of socialism. Social psychologists have explained the nature of the process which we are here dealing with. A feeling of insecurity – which can be objectively, historically conditioned or can be created or supported by bolstering propaganda – leads to powerful affective identification of the masses with a leader and to their readiness to follow him blindly, fanatically. In this way, one arrives at the point of a clear-cut regression and depersonalisation of the individual. Instead of growing progressively and becoming more individualised, the individual forgets himself, his needs and his potentialities, his living projects, he frees himself from personal responsibility and becomes an element of the masses which completely, uncritically and irrationally adapts itself to the mood of the leader.

This analysis shows that in post-capitalist society which evolves towards socialism, powerful and drastic forms of political alienation are possible to the extent to which the revolutionary élite turns itself into a bureaucracy, and to the extent to which a division of people into political subjects and political objects occurs.


## 2   The essence of bureaucracy

This is a notion which in its application to the society of a transition period has undoubtedly undergone a degree of generalisation. In a capitalist society, bureaucracy is the apparatus of the expert, of the executor, and to a greater or lesser extent it can be identified with the social group which constitutes the State apparatus and wields executive power. Both Marx and Lenin – the former in his analysis of the civil war in France, the latter more particularly in his later writings – were very much aware of the danger that, following successful political revolutions, a new bureaucracy forms itself from the ranks of the leaders of the victorious working class. However after the death of Lenin, Stalin very soon shifted the meaning of the term. From now on 'bureaucratic' came to be used only for the definitely cold, superior, routine, formalistic relationship of some functionaries towards ordinary people and their problems.

Not until Stalinism was opened to criticism was the problem of bureaucracy properly identified as the problem of monopolisation of political power. However all the maze of different opinions, critical of Stalinism had weaknesses of their own. The very concept of bureaucracy was never explained in a satisfactory way. In addition, bureaucracy and bureaucratic tendencies were often vehemently discussed by those who are themselves, to a marked degree, bureaucrats, so that one not infrequently gains the impression that bureaucracy has become a phantom force against which everybody is striving, but which it is quite impossible to locate.

On the other hand, in widening the concept of bureaucracy, it is possible to go so far in the other direction that it sometimes becomes identified with any social group which guides and regulates the social processes. In this sense, then, it has been stated that politics itself gives birth to bureaucracy, and that bureaucracy is necessarily connected with the existence of the function of centralised planning in society. Here the ideas of *politics, centralisation,* and *planning* are treated in an oversimplified way. Any developed society needs regulative and directive functions at the level of the global society.

Those who perform these functions do not fall by virtue of *this itself* into bureaucracy. In this sense we can distinguish the politics of self-government and bureaucratic politics. In reality, *political bureaucracy is a permanent and coherent social group which occupies itself professionally with politics, which has escaped the control of the people and which, thanks to unlimited power in the distribution of the past, embodied labour, secures lesser or greater material privileges to itself.*  Each of these three conditions is necessary but all taken together constitute a sufficient condition for the existence of bureaucracy.

1 The professionalisation of politics is the first step towards the creation of an isolated, closed and, in relation to the rest of society, a very coherent social stratum. In this sense bureaucracy is that social stratum which longs to hold permanently to the principle of partiality which in the process of revolution had already begun to be surpassed. After the destruction of the bourgeoisie as a class, all the social strata except the bureaucracy are interested in ensuring that political activity is general,

public life open to all, and that it should be moral, just, philosophically thought-out, and scientifically based; in other words, that instead of being a particular, partial sphere of social consciousness and activity, it becomes a *moment* of integral, rational and human practice. Bureaucracy is the material bearer of the isolation and partiality of politics, and this is why it resists so bitterly all tendencies to supersede traditional professional politics as a sphere of alienation.

2 The process of withdrawal and isolation of the bureaucracy from the people in whose name it rules lies in the fact that elections become a pure form, that the bureaucracy transforms the responsibility of the electors into responsibility to party forums, and that the electors lose the power to replace their representatives for the simple reason that they are atomised, isolated one from another, and as individual units are quite powerless. In all the key economic and political processes in such a society, the greatest numbers of people find themselves permanently in the position of the *objects* of history. They are the mass which gives necessary, material energy to the realisation of the apparently collective will mediated by the bureaucracy. Indeed under such circumstances the bureaucracy is the sole historic subject. Far from being that part of the proletariat in which the collective will of the proletariat arrives at a self-conscious and practical fulfilment, the bureaucracy ensures that the proletariat and the other mass of society accept its personal will as its own and thus become instruments of its practical realisation. This is the highest form of 'cunning subtlety of mind': people, who normally have their own purpose, act in a depersonalised way – as 'things' – in order to fulfil an exterior bureaucratic purpose. This is the highest and most subtle form of reification: never have people been so successfully manipulated, thanks, among other things, to the extraordinary technical perfection of all forms and methods of propaganda. Never have so few people been aware that they are being treated as things. Because of this, bureaucracy is the bearer of the principle of *reification* in a society which has already begun to create essential preconditions for its surpassing in the sphere of politics.

3 Bureaucracy has full monopoly in deciding on the distribution and use of the past, embodied labour. It usually uses this monopoly to secure for itself various material privileges.

As a social stratum the bureaucracy recruits its members from the ranks of people who no longer have any humanistic ideals, and whose human needs have remained very undeveloped. The need to possess social power is the fundamental life-need of the bureaucrat. But power demands, among other things, an unlimited disposal of things – the most expensive car, the most stylish furniture, etc. All these are to the bureaucrat, above all, symbols of his social status, of the degree of his power. Having originally developed very indirectly, the impulse to ownership can become the dominant motive in the second generation of bureaucrats. What was at the beginning a typically ideological attitude – an attempt to rationalise and justify the relationship of exploitation which at first was not yet clear even to the bureaucrat himself – later becomes a clearly cynical and hypocritical attitude. One no longer believes one's own words, but uses them for pragmatic reasons, in order to conceal truth deliberately. So it becomes evident that in order to supersede exploitation it is not sufficient merely to destroy the private ownership of the means of production. As long as relatively undeveloped productive powers and relative material shortages produce the impulse for the possession of ever better material goods, and as long as a particular social group has a monopoly of decision-making over embodied labour, it is possible for that group to use a considerable part of the social surplus value for its own personal appetites and not for the general social needs. So bureaucracy is the bearer of the principle of *exploitation* in a society in which all other exploitatory social groups have been abolished.

The concept of bureaucracy which has been given here is a theoretical one. In a simplified way it designates a developed, full limit-form of something which in reality is found in varying degrees of growth, or which possesses only some of these characteristics. Therefore, when we are concerned with the concrete empirical reality of a given country, we shall need to speak sometimes of the tendency towards bureaucratisation, and of the fact that certain individuals are bureaucrats to the degree to which their behaviour corresponds to these patterns.

It would be mistaken to identify bureaucracy with a stratum of professional politicians in a socialist society. There are also bureaucrats among the leaders and organisers in the fields of economics, science, and the arts. In addition, there are politicians who contribute to surpassing bureaucracy by the progressive realisation of a system of self-government, just as there are some political leaders in whom the revolutionary and the bureaucrat are locked in combat.

On the other hand, there is no reason to differentiate strictly between political leadership and bureaucracy and to reduce the latter to the executive apparatus of government. Under definite social conditions, which have been specified in the foregoing exposition, the notion of bureaucracy must be applied in such a way as to embrace both.

## 3　The meaning of self-government

Self-government is the dialectical negation of State socialism with its inherent tendencies towards bureaucratisation.

However, self-government cannot be reduced to its initial historical forms which at present exist in Yugoslavia. This means, first of all, that it cannot be limited only to production relations at the level of the enterprise and to the local organs of social power. The complete and definitive surpassing of bureaucracy is possible only when self-government reaches the top: when the central organs of the State are converted into organs of self-government. Secondly, even if self-government is primarily an economic and political phenomenon it is not only that. It is a concept which embraces the whole of social life, which has a range of technical, social, psychological and cultural presuppositions and consequences. Behind it stands a radically different, new concept of society and of man, a whole new structure of philosophical assumptions, radically opposed to that by which bureaucracy tries to rationalise its existence.

We can begin an explicit formulation of this philosophical structure with an analysis of the concept of self-government itself.

Self-government means that the functions of directing social processes are no longer performed by forces outside the mass of society, opposed to it, but in the hands of the very same people who produce, who create social life in all its

forms. Self-government means the supersession of the permanent and fixed division of society into the subjects and the
objects of history, into rulers and executors, into the cunning
social mind and its physical instruments in human form.

The idea of government which has been used here means, in
the context of Marx's humanistic thought, *rational* and
*revolutionary* government. It is *rational* in the sense that it is
based on an objective critical analysis of existing reality, on a
knowledge of the real possibilities of its change, on a choice of
those real possibilities which are optimal in relation to the
given end.

The fundamental end which serves as the main criterion of
rational decision-making in the process of government is the
*abolition of all forms of human oppression and poverty and the freeing
of every individual to a full rich life in a really human community*.
This aim is *revolutionary*, and so is the whole of government,
which takes on its meaning in relation to this aim. The concern
is not, however with any 'total revolution' in an absolute
historical meaning of the word. The aim is fully determined
historically by the given forms of human needs and human
wants. It is 'fundamental' or 'ultimate' only in relation to the
given historical epoch. However being aware of this and
knowing the real situation in society at a given historical
moment is a sufficient condition for being able to determine
the next practical steps, and to give a revolutionary impetus to
our practice.

Of course, self-government does not mean that every individual takes part directly in government at all levels. Such
direct self-government is possible only in the basic social
organisations – enterprises, communes, cultural institutions,
etc. Self-government means that the functions of government
in the broader social organisations are performed in turn by
competent, freely-elected individuals who factually express
the interests of the people and whose functions cannot bring
them, even temporarily, any material privileges, any superior
status in society – nothing but confidence, respect and love. In
a society in which self-government is growing, the criterion of
the personal abilities of the candidate – his mind, his knowledge, his moral integrity, his skill – come increasingly to
expression. In bureaucratic society the function of ruling has
endowed definite authority. Here people must first win

authority in order to get the honour of performing a political function.

Such a view of rational and revolutionary self-government implies a radical reappraisal of the concept of politics. Not only are politics no longer the concern of a single personal profession, they are no longer an isolated, partial, social activity. The gradual abolition of practicism, of frequent amorality, of the improvisatory character of politics now begin to take place. Politics is being given an awareness of the basic revolutionary aims by humanistic philosophy; politics is now becoming *philosophical*. Knowledge of the real situation and tendencies of change is provided by science; politics is becoming *scientific*. In order to apply means which are adequate to ends, political behaviour must conform to defined moral norms which, for their part, correspond to basic accepted human values; politics are now becoming *moral*. They are also beginning to become an art – *sui generis* – for there is no reason why in this field, beauty, nobility and a feeling of dignity should not be preferred to greyness of thought and rawness of behaviour.

Such a process of the totalisation of social consciousness is parallel to the process of the simultaneous individualisation and socialisation of man. Both presuppose a technically highly developed and rich society in which the elementary material needs of people are satisfied, in which genuine culture has come within the reach of all, and in which there exist sufficiently strong forces, which in the name of a critical and humanistic self-consciousness unceasingly lay down the demand for the dialectical supersession of every existing historical form.

It is an irony of history that self-government first began to be realised in a relatively backward semi-rural country, and not in the highly developed and relatively rich social communities of the West. From this it follows that, on the one hand, self-government in Yugoslavia will not be fully realised, and its forms be fulfilled by the corresponding content, for a long time. On the other hand, absence of self-government in the West may be explained by the absence of a powerful critical humanistic conscious factor, such as would be able to lead the whole of society to the realisation of its optimal historical possibilities.

What is essential for Marxist theory is the thesis of the *objective possibility of self-government*, and not of its necessary realisation. The very idea of self-government presupposes that people themselves are the creators of history in given conditions, i.e. in the objectively determined framework of possibilities. In this way, the idea of self-government presupposes an open, activist interpretation of history in which the artificial gap between law and contingency, necessity and freedom has been overcome. The philosophy of bureaucracy is essentially different in this respect. Bureaucracy advocates voluntarism when the question is of the future, and it predates absolute determinism when the question is of the past. As it does not have scientific knowledge itself, as it does not even have sufficient confidence in the scientist, finally since the most rational decisions, most adequate to the expected course of things, would often be against its own interests, bureaucracy does not even try to justify rationally its projects for the future, but at best gives them the necessary authority by quoting classical texts. But this is why it gives an aura of necessity to everything that happened in the past. In both cases the key concept of *real possibility* has no meaning. History is assumed to be a linear process from which bureaucracy never deviates.

But if history is an open and multilinear process in which nothing is guaranteed and completely provided for in advance, we are faced with the question: cannot self-government lead to chaos and disintegration, to a state of restless change, to a bad and irrational solution to the key questions of society? Such a course is not only a possibility but a necessity in the opinion of the bureaucrat. From here comes his historical responsibility for the further course of building socialism. From this there follows not only a lack of confidence in the intelligentsia but also an aristocratic attitude towards the working class and towards people in general. Whenever it speaks of the people, bureaucracy regards them basically as a primitive, backward mass, which, without its rule, would become quite savage and destroy all that has been gained by revolution. In the last analysis it would seem to follow that the building of socialism is a type of enforced happiness, in which the man who is making someone happy never stops speaking and acting in the name of the man who is made happy.

Finally, one of the most essential differences in the

philosophical assumptions of bureaucracy and self-government is their respective attitudes to dialectics. Bureaucracy often makes use of the formulae of dialectics. Apart from this it makes considerable efforts to give an appearance of permanent dialectical movement and perfection to the society which it controls. It makes use of a vast amount of activity in thinking out new social forms, new institutional frameworks, new programmes. These forms and institutions are changed even before they have been properly tried, programmes are 'surpassed' even before they can be realised in practice. This pseudo-dialectics goes together with a very decisive denial of dialectics in all essential things. Dialectic unity of the opposites is turned into 'monolithic unity'. Contradictions are denied and concealed. Philosophers, scientists and artists are expected, above all, to confirm the present State, to look for the positive in it. Public criticism is usually treated as a kind of petty bourgeois confusion, and is often blocked in the most brutal way.

In complete contrast, self-government presupposes dialectics to such an extent that it could be regarded as political dialectics in practice. Self-government is a particular form of self-movement. Thus the struggle of different tendencies, opinions and projects is presupposed, although in a highly developed society these tensions and conflicts gain a more humane form and resolve themselves in a more humane way. So we are concerned with a society which is pluralistic, in which there are many different groups and communities, but in which the degree of socialisation has advanced so far, in which certain values are already so widely accepted that there is no longer any need for violence to be used to preserve its integrity. Public social criticism is now the most efficient means of surpassing the limitations of every existing social form.

When we fully understand social self-government it becomes clear that its introduction really is a fundamental social revolution and also that it must be construed as a long-lasting historical process and not a sudden transmutation.

# 3 Revolutionary Social Change

## 1 The concept of a social revolution

There are two basic distinctions among various types of social change which are relevant to the explication of the concept of a social revolution. One is the distinction between mere *modifications* and *structural transformations* of a given society. What is presupposed here is that we know what are the defining characteristics of the type of social system to which that particular society belongs. Each defining characteristic is a *necessary* condition, all of them are a *sufficient* condition for belonging to a certain social type such as feudalism or capitalism. Social change that does not affect any defining characteristics is a modification. When at least one has been abolished we are in the presence of a structural transformation which can be more or less complete. (In this sense we may speak of a revolution as a historical process, and of its incompleteness.) The product of an incomplete revolution is a hybrid social system: feudal–capitalist or capitalist–socialist. When a revolutionary process comes to its end we have an entirely new type of society with new defining characteristics.

Another essential distinction among various kinds of social changes is between a *progressive* (emancipatory) and a *retrogressive* change. These are, admittedly, value-laden concepts. A theory of revolution that uses them is not reduced to a mere description, analysis and explanation of actual social changes. The latter approach is obviously uncritical and could be used for ideological purposes: for example, when some scholars interpret changes introduced by Stalin in Soviet society between 1929 and 1936 as a 'revolution from above', then this either helps to support the myth of merely another phase of the continuous Soviet socialist revolution begun in 1917 (which serves the purposes of Stalinist propaganda), or denigrates the really emancipatory early phase of the October Revolution by this identification (which serves the purposes of right-wing propaganda). Definitions are, of course, a matter of convention, but conventions are not value-free. By blurring important distinctions or by focusing on them, semantic conventions may mystify or demystify reality to which our terms refer.

A social change will therefore be considered *revolutionary* when it satisfies two conditions discussed above: it is a progressive (emancipatory) structural transformation. This concept of social revolution is not only opposed to a broad, neutral, descriptive characterisation of any sudden, violent social change, as 'revolutionary', it is also incompatible with an *a priori* transcendental postulation of revolution devoid of any historical substance. Social revolution is a historical category; each of its particular types (bourgeois, socialist revolution) is relative to a definite historical epoch and constitutes an optimal real possibility of change of a definite social system in that epoch.

A critical theory of revolution of this type presupposes two basic philosophical criteria:

1  A criterion of distinguishing between a structural transformation and modification.
2  A criterion of distinguishing between the progressive and the regressive.

As we shall see, these two philosophical assumptions are closely related.

1  The idea of a structural transformation is involved in the dialectical category of *transcendence* (*Aufhebung*). It is assumed that we already know what are the necessary structural characteristics of the initial form (system or, in Marx's terminology, a socio-economic formation). When a form (system) exhausts its possibilities of development and finds itself in crisis, its necessary characteristics become inner limitations, the barriers for further development. To transcend such a form means practically to abolish its inner limitations, to preserve all those features which constitute indispensable conditions for further development and to create a new superior form (superior from our basic standpoint of evaluation).

Thus necessary characteristics of capitalism are a wasteful, exponentially growing commodity production; private property of the means of production, which involves economic exploitation; State coercion as a means of class domination, egoism, competition and increasing consumption as basic motives of all activity. These characteristics prove more and more to be limits of any further historical progress. To revolutionise bourgeois society means to abolish those limits, but at the same time to preserve all those achievements of the centuries-long struggle for human emancipation which constitute the necessary ground for any further evolution. Only when a certain level of material and cultural development has already been reached (a level of technology and human productive power, of human rights, of social collaboration and of universal cultural values) does it become historically possible to build a new, more free and a more just socialist society.

2 The category of transcendence involves a basic criterion of evaluation that allows us to distinguish between the positive and the negative, between the progressive and the regressive. We have seen in Chapter 1 that Marxist humanism rests on the idea of man as a being of praxis. Since this idea holds universally (each individual has a potential for praxis), and since praxis is essentially free and creative i.e. a self-determining activity, it follows that a principle of *equal self-determination* constitutes that philosophical criterion which makes all evaluation of social phenomena possible. This principle asserts two things. First, as a matter of fact, each human individual has a capacity of self-determination, i.e. the capacity to choose autonomously among alternatives, to transcend habitual patterns and act in a new, creative way. Second, since all individuals are endowed with this specifically human potential, they should be equally treated as self-determining beings.

Thus to say that a social change is progessive and emancipatory means that, on the one hand, it increases the degree of human self-determination, and, on the other hand, it makes it more universal, more equally realised.

Equal self-determination has a number of practical, socially relevant implications which are more or less incompatible with present-day institutions and patterns of social life of either liberalist 'free world', or State-socialist 'soviet' society.

First, such implication is that members of society must decide themselves (directly or indirectly, through their elected and responsible delegates) about all matters of common interest. This rules out any social structure in which decision-making is a monopoly of any particular group, alienated from the rest of society, that pursues its own particular interests (such as feudal nobility, royal dynasty, capital, State bureaucracy, the Church, the ruling party).

Second, self-determination as a social principle presupposes a social order which is not only not heteronomously regulated, but is also not too strictly regulated. Life in any community involves some constraints, but these must be not only democratically accepted but also, whenever possible, flexible enough to allow alternatives among which to choose, and decisions from which individuals and minorities may dissent.

Third, alternatives must not only exist objectively, but be known, deliberated, and critically evaluated. In most countries the law offers all kinds of favourable legal possibilities to all citizens, but most ordinary citizens are ignorant of them – in practice, they are open only to those who can afford to buy expert legal advice. Awareness of economic, political, cultural possibilities requires an extensive and complex, reliable knowledge of the situation, of its scarcities and limitations, of existing trends, of conflicts to be solved, of the psychological dispositions of other people. Freedom is incompatible with ignorance, biased or utterly distorted perception of reality. If there are social élites which have a privileged access to information, the majority will be deprived of determining power.

Fourth, true autonomy of choice may go together with equality of self-determination only if two other conditions are met. One is *pluralism* – recognition of different groups and sub-groups with different interests, ethnic backgrounds, cultural traditions, conscious goals and aspirations. The other is *open, unhindered* flow of information, exchange of ideas, expression of critical views, formation of general will and of a powerful public opinion through dialogue and the struggle of opposite opinions.

Fifth, since self-determination involves action that accords to autonomous choice and brings to life potential creative abilities of the given subject, building up a society on the basis of this principle would require a radical restructuring of all social practice, especially of work. Alienated labour would have to be resolutely reduced and completely eliminated wherever possible; socially necessary work would have to be freely elected and tend to become an end in itself. Politics as well as culture would lose its exclusive, élitist character and would turn into fields of activity where each individual would be able fully to express himself.

Sixth, equal self-determination cannot possibly mean merely 'everybody's doing his own thing'; conflict and cancelling out of mutually exclusive actions of different unrelated individuals would result in general frustration and emergence of unintended, undesirable consequences. The whole process would have a blind deterministic character, indistinguishable from that in unorganic nature. Self-determination as a social process presupposes, therefore, a high level of co-ordination and conscious rational direction of social activities.

Seventh, equal self-determination as a general principle of society implies a process of education which is radically different from the kind of socialisation that takes place in a reified society. Its task would have to be to prepare a young individual for autonomous choice, for creative work, for meaningful communication and unselfish collaboration with other members of society. The basic purpose of education would be the discovery of a person's true self of his true needs, and of his capacities for praxis.

## 2   Basic issues of a socialist revolution

Socialist revolution *may* – but *need not* – *be violent*. It may also – but need not – have the character of a *sudden, eruptive* change. Certain of Marx's well-known general formulations contributed to the identification of socialist revolution with a dramatic, inevitable, violent collapse of capitalism. This became a dogma of the Second International. Revolution was construed as a cataclysm in the future for which the workers' movement ought to prepare. This view was challenged by Bernstein's reformism which, in spite of its plain opportunism, contained one sound implicit idea: the movement must not be separated from the revolutionary *telos* in future; it cannot be reduced only to preparatory work, reforms achieved by the movement must themselves have revolutionary character. On the other hand, Rosa Luxemburg improved the objectivist view of the social-democratic centre by her concept of revolution as 'a continual chain of political and social catastrophes and convulsions which, combined with periodical economic catastrophes in the form of crises, will prevail the continuation of capitalist accumulation . . . even before capitalism reaches the natural limits of its economic development'.[1] The conceptual difficulty here is that when a collapse or catastrophe is not understood as one event, but as a series of events, a series of convulsions and catastrophes, it may not be possible to establish the difference between such a catastrophic event and an ordinary event: the concept of catastrophe becomes unclear. Its use expresses only the need to emphasise discontinuity between two phases of development. And this discontinuity is most clearly expressed by the idea of a *structural transformation*, replacement of a certain socio-economic formation by another essentially different one. Discontinuity need not have the form of a collapse, of a destruction of one system and a building of another on its ruins. It may also have the form of a series of gradual, continuous changes, which in its totality constitutes the transition from one system to another. This is the idea of revolutionary reformism which will be discussed later.

Socialist revolution cannot be reduced to seizure of political power, to political revolution. Political revolution is only one dimension (or even an 'episode' in Marx's words). Furthermore, political revolution cannot be reduced to a mere abolition of the political power of the bourgeoisie and building of new forms of workers' democracy (which Marx called, very inadequately, 'dictatorship of the proletariat'). Political revolution is the whole process of abolition of the division of society into a political and a civil society, abolition of politics as a particular social sphere in which struggle for power takes place and in which a minority of professional – the exclusive political *subject* – rules over a majority of people who are reduced to mere *objects* of politics. This implies that political revolution embraces the whole long process of superseding the State – that form of political organisation which rests on coercion, and serves as the instrument of class domination. This also implies a transcendence of the institutions of representative, parliamentary democracy, and of political parties, a specifically bourgeois form of political organisation characterised by struggle for power, authoritarian decision-making, hierarchy and ideological manipulation of the masses. The State is replaced by a network of self-governing bodies at all levels of social organisation; representative democracy is replaced by a participatory one which maximally engages all citizens in social decision-making. Political parties lose, in this way, the role of mediators between State power and the people, and are replaced by new forms of political organisation aimed primarily at political education and the formation of public opinion of particular social groups.

Another dimension of socialist revolution is economic. It involves much more than usually conceived abolition of private property. It means also transcendence of commodity production, of the anarchy of the market, of exploitation, class domination and authoritarian, economic decision-making, of alienated labour.

Private property is not only the possessed object – a machine, a pile of commodities, money – but also a specific, typically bourgeois attitude toward the world for which it is characteristic that 'all human senses are reduced to a sense of *having*', and that one can enjoy objects and human beings only when they are possessed. Private ownership of the means of production cannot be abolished by a simple 'nationalisation', turning those means into State property. The social élite that has a monopoly of State power has thereby an almost unlimited power of disposal with the 'nationalised' means of production. It also has a socially unrecognised but practically existing right to appropriate a substantial part of the social surplus-value in the form of various privileges. These are obviously some of the essential functions of property. Private property may really be transcended only in a society which is no longer organised as a State, and where politics has indeed become open to all citizens. Genuinely socialised property presupposes an integral self-government at the level of global society. Only then does it become possible to direct rationally production toward satisfaction of human needs; only then compulsion and exploitation give way to self-governing decision-making about the surplus of social work. The end result of economic revolution is the disappearance of classes and class conflicts, although not of many other conceivable kinds of conflicts among groups with different particular interests.

A specific aspect of economic revolution is *technological revolution*. This means not only accelerated quantitative growth of productive forces, but also their qualitative change.

Official Marxist theory has onesidedly emphasised the former. At an early phase of its development, the new socialist society *in statu nescendi* has to wrestle with poverty and intolerably long hours of work for the working class. Simple increase of productive powers meets the basic needs of all individuals and allows reduction of working hours. However it has often been overlooked that certain technologies and forms of productive organisation turn work into a profoundly alienating activity independent of the social system. If the basic emancipatory substance of socialism is the struggle against all forms of alienation, efforts must be made to change the whole organisation of work qualitatively, and to choose among alternative technologies those which are less dehumanising, even if they are less efficient.

Political and economic revolution cannot go very far without *cultural revolution*. New socialist culture presupposes new critical consciousness, new value orientation, a new life-style, a new sensibility in human relationships. The socialisation process in the family and in the school requires a radical restructuring. Patriarchal obedience and subservience, a characteristically bourgeois motivation to succeed at any price, a hedonistic mentality of the *homo consumens* must be replaced by a spirit of freedom, creativity, personal dignity and human solidarity. A new generation of parents and teachers educated in this new spirit must grow before one can ascertain that changes of political institutions and patterns of work have indeed been followed by changes in human relations and life-style.

Vulgar Marxism postulates that, in opposition to bourgeois revolution, socialist revolution must start with political, continue with economic, and end up with cultural revolution. Recent history has shown conclusively that such a scheme was entirely inadequate. A political revolution that does not develop new human relationships and a new culture – parallel to abolition of economic exploitation and of the bourgeois style of life, is doomed to failure, and sometimes to monstrous deformation.

One of the most controversial issues of the theory of socialist revolution is the problem of its historical subject. The classical view of the proletariat as the subject of revolution is in crisis 1) after a series of anti-capitalist, twentieth-century revolutions, in which the decisive role was played by the peasants; and 2) in the absence of revolution in developed industrial countries. Marx's theory must be supplemented, and in some senses transcended.

Anti-capitalist revolutions are possible in under-developed societies because a parasitic bourgeoisie can neither secure a satisfactory growth rate nor protect the vital interests of that country. Such a weak, impotent bourgeois class usually enters alliances with feudal lords or with the more powerful bourgeoisie of the world's superpowers, against its own people. In such situations peasantry, interested in agrarian reform and national independence, can play a decisive revolutionary role.

And yet in the whole epoch of the crisis and transcendence of capitalism the most important potential subject of revolutionary changes is the working class, in the broad sense of that term. It is true that if the working class is reduced to manual workers only – immediate producers – it constitutes only a minority, and a decreasing section of the total labour force in developed industrial societies. However, such a reduction no longer makes any sense. Employees in the services – teachers, technicians and all those who live by their work and not on their property – who produce but do not appropriate the surplus work of others, who are the obvious victims of alienated labour, all objectively belong to the working class, no matter how they perceive their social position and whether they prefer to regard themselves as workers or as the middle class.

The material standard of living of workers has greatly improved in this century, and some workers can no longer be considered proletarian: they may own some stock, and live a double existence of workers/petty bourgeois. And yet the vast majority of workers can still be motivated to revolutionary activity because of certain features of their social position:

1 A considerable number of the working class still suffers from material misery, unemployment and total exclusion from social life. It suffers *in toto* from spiritual pauperism. Even in the most developed bourgeois societies it has an extremely limited access to true cultural values.

2 The consequence of a fast growth of the productivity of labour and much lower increase of workers' wages is a growing degree of exploitation.

3 The working class is still either completely excluded from

the process of decision-making, or it participates (often in a symbolic way and without decision-making power) on the minor, inessential issues of production and distribution.

4 Work is still extremely dehumanised. Alienated labour cannot be transcended within the framework of production for profits.

5 Workers are, to a much greater extent than the rest of population, the victims of pollution and depletion of natural environment. These are the consequences of the exponential growth of capitalist societies, and may be overcome only by abolition of the production for profit.

The revolutionary potential of the working class does not only follow from the objective characteristic of its social position, but also from the psychological fact that the worker sells to his employer only his labour and not his whole personality – as do the diplomat, journalist, and intellectual conformist. He has, therefore, a chance of preserving his independence, critical spirit and human dignity. Whether this chance is realised, in spite of the enormous pressure from the mass media on his consciousness, depends on whether the working-class intelligentsia (each class has its own intelligentsia!) succeeds in creating the basic elements of a new revolutionary culture. The key element is the critical consciousness of the real social position of the working class, and the optimal historical possibilities of its emancipation. The role of intellectuals is not to introduce this consciousness into the working class 'from outside' in a mechanical, authoritarian way. Their task is rather to express in a concise articulate, theoretically well-grounded way what the workers feel intuitively and recognise as their vital interests. The revolutionary intelligentsia, which creates such a critical consciousness, which lives on its work, and which is itself oppressed and exploited, is a part of the working class, not a self-appointed, alienated vanguard.

The experience of all known, incomplete, socialist revolutions is that the revolutionary vanguard tends to turn into a new ruling élite, a political bureaucracy, if:

– an authoritarian, hierarchical political party has hegemony in the revolutionary movement;

– leadership of the movement is glorified rather than watched critically, controlled and rotated from time to time;

– revolutionary theory turns into a dogmatic official ideology, the purpose of which is legitimisation of the new order.

A socialist revolution may be completed without pathological deformation only by a mass movement which preserves an inner democratic structure, and enough space for a plurality of interests and views within a framework of common revolutionary goals; which keeps its leaders responsible to the movement, recallable and exposed to criticism; whose theory never ceases to develop a critical consciousness of the movement about itself.

The presuppositions of such a broad democratic revolutionary movement are a profound crisis of capitalist society; a minimum of political democracy and protection of civil rights; and a high level of socialist enlightenment.

## 3   The character of the present day crisis of private and State capitalism

A historical situation may be characterised as a situation of crisis when there are incompatibilities between the structural characteristics of existing social forms and the recognised needs of individuals to survive and develop as emancipated, self-determining human beings.

A critical humanist analysis of the present day world's crises leads to the identification of the following six crucial problems: material and spiritual poverty; destruction of communities; alienated labour; authoritarian socialisation; bureaucratisation; ecological degradation.

1 *Poverty* still exists despite impressive economic development during recent decades. Its forms are drastic in many Third World countries which suffer not only from extremely low productivity of labour and gross inequality in the distribution of wealth, but also from wasteful government policies, which follow those of the developed, industrial countries, and try to catch up thereby decreasing employment possibilities. As a consequence, the conditions of the poorest get worse, even in absolute terms, and millions may starve in coming years. Poverty could disappear in wealthy Western countries with an average $6000–$7000 national *per capita* income. For the first time in history it is possible to satisfy the basic needs of

each individual (needs for food, housing, basic education, health protection, etc.). In some Northern European countries the problem of material poverty has indeed nearly been solved. In other wealthy countries like the United States about one-fifth of the population still lives under conditions of both material and spiritual misery: inadequately fed, in slums, permanently unemployed, without health protection, socially discriminated against, especially when they belong to racial minorities.

A specific form of poverty is *spiritual pauperism* – a complete exclusion from the world of knowledge and culture even of those who enjoy a satisfactory material standard of living. Spiritual pauperism is the result of poor education, too long hours of stultifying work, and cheap mind-killing entertainment offered by commercialised mass media.

2 *Disintegration of communities* is a necessary consequence of an economic arrangement that makes permanent competition and conflict indispensable, and pushes individuals toward increasing privatisation. As a surrogate, illusory communities are formed on the basis of shared religious faith, 'national interest', and hatred of ideological enemies. With the decline of religion, awakening from aggressive patriotism and ideological disillusionment, disintegrative forces tend to prevail over integrative ones. An extreme example is the threatened economic breakdown of principal American cities, and an exodus to the suburbs which do not satisfy even the minimal criteria to be considered communities. Another large-scale phenomenon is the breaking up of a society into ethnic groups, which in turn break down into family groups, which are, on their part, shattered by the conflict of generations and sexes. In spite of his overwhelmingly strong need to belong to a genuine community, to be recognised and understood by others, modern man appears to be condemned to hopeless loneliness.

One aspect of the problem is the destruction of real, meaningful communication. Closed within the walls of the nuclear family, the child has little chance to associate with older generations and members of extended families. No matter how well sheltered and over-protected the child may be, the chances are that there will not be many hours when he will have the undivided attention of his parents and their eagerness to talk, and play. There might be a lot of co-existence in the same physical space, but very little contact in the same psychological space.

The loneliness of adults is even worse – the child may at least have brothers and sisters. Most life-styles in developed industrial society are adverse to the development of genuine, spontaneous bonds between people: work demands full concentration all the time; extremely passive leisure is filled with meaningless mass media contents; communication in political life turns into double-talk, and parties become places in which to show off and sell oneself. The emptier the life the more shallow and mindless the means of communication.

3 *Work*, that still occupies the major part of active life in spite of the enormous increase of productive power, is extremely alienated. The recent history of labour for the vast majority of ordinary people reveals the destruction of any trace of creativity which existed in the work of the artisan and the farmer. In modern industry work is mechanical, monotonous and depersonalised. Human beings are assigned fixed roles in the process of production, and have little chance of escaping from the narrow world of their professional specialty for the rest of their life. The whole of production is geared to increasing efficiency and profitability, rather than to augmenting the satisfaction of genuine human needs. The worker is totally isolated from the goals of the working organisation to which he belongs. He experiences his activity as meaningless and merely instrumental, and himself as powerless to change anything in the structure of the production process.

Alienation in labour rose sharply with the introduction of the assembly-line technology, especially in the automobile industry. It tends to decrease with automated industry but is still a very widespread phenomenon.

4 The counterpart of alienation is growing *bureaucratisation*. In spite of great and very real differences between political institutions of oligarchic and liberal societies, most people are excluded from active participation in social decision-making. In systems of representative democracy civil liberties are better protected than in any other existing political structure. And yet the growing role of the State in the economy and public welfare has resulted in a quickly expanding bureaucracy, and in abuse of power and corruption. New bureaucracy emerging

in contemporary forms of Statism is more powerful and dangerous that the old Weberian bureaucracy. Bureaucracy in the Weberian sense played a strictly instrumental role. It served either the elected representatives (in liberal societies) or the royal house (in autocratic States such as the Habsburg's Austro-Hungary and the Tsar's Russia). It was rational, in the sense of technical rationality: its aims were strictly regulated and predictable. The growing power of the State in the twentieth century creates increasing scope for a new type of bureaucracy which pretends to lead and to rule rather than merely to serve. This bureaucracy, being in control of huge, political machinery and of mass media, is usually devoid of any sense of responsibility to the electorate which characterised the bourgeois democratic leaders of the nineteenth century. It also lacks a sense of nobility, honour and good taste, which distinguished enlightened absolute monarchs in the seventeenth and eighteenth centuries.

The distance between citizen and centres of power has increased not only because of the hypertrophy of these centres but also because of the strengthening of the self-appointed mediators – power-hungry political parties. Parties, as they emerged in the nineteenth century, are not organisations whose function is merely to express clearly and promote a particular public interest; they tend to win power and to rule in place of those whose support they enjoy. They are hierarchical, with their own bosses, professional functionaries and masses; they practise more or less authoritarian procedures of decision-making and a heteronomous discipline. They rationalise their particular interests, build up appropriate ideologies and propagate biased and distorted images of reality. Use of powerful mass media for ideological manipulation makes individual citizens even more inept and impotent.

5 A striking feature of modern life is the absence of serious widespread and sustained resistance to either alienated labour or to growing bureaucratisation. The counter-culture movement in recent years looks harmless in comparison with the struggle for land, for political liberties, and for higher wages in the late feudal and early capitalist societies. The opposition to increasing State control is stronger from a conservative, *laissez-faire* point of view than from the standpoint of participatory democracy. The reluctance to rebel against the

alienating aspects of present day economic and political institutions is not only the consequence of the overwhelming strength of these institutions and of the widespread conviction that, no matter how unpleasant, they are inevitable and representative of modern times. It is rather the result of a certain kind of authoritarian individuality-killing socialisation which does not even allow consciousness of the problem, let alone rebellion against obvious folly. Wilhelm Reich was one of the first to realise that the evil is not only in the institutions but also in the basic dispositions of little men, educated in authoritarian families and schools.

All socialisation has always involved an authoritarian, individuality-suppressing, life-killing element. And yet this has never been done in such a large-scale, systematic, organised way. Accelerated material progress awakens growing aspirations which frustrated adults project onto their children. From the start the young generation is subject to a drill – first at home then in the school – with a double purpose: to be turned into disciplined performers in the professional division of work and into loyal citizens of the State. It goes without saying that the drill does not always succeed – another indication that human beings do have a latent disposition to escape full, external determination and to be free. On the other hand, the remarkable success of *authoritarian socialisation* shows how adaptable men are and how grave is the ever-present danger of losing oneself. Without a radical change of both the goals and institutions of education, all other social changes would succeed only superficially, without changing human motives, attitudes and relationships.

6 Capitalism and State-socialism share an overriding interest in maximising expansion of material production. The ruling élites in the Third World exhibit a psychological propensity to catch up with the already reached international level. In all these cases the development of productive forces is construed as a purely quantitative growth. At the same time, when we know how scarce and irrevocably limited certain natural materials and energy sources are, and how dangerously disturbed are certain natural harmonies indispensable for life, an exponentially growing industry continues to increase its output, to create artificial needs, and to encourage a wasteful consumption of these very scarce resources. This is a

universal problem, although the degree of pollution and depletion may vary considerably. We all live on the same planet, are
victims of the same ideology of unlimited expansion, and
suffer from consequences which can no longer be localised.

It is possible to begin to attack those problems one by one,
but not to solve them separately from each other. Material
poverty may be overcome within a very authoritarian society,
but spiritual pauperism will increase. Participatory democracy
does not make much sense without a fundamental redistribution of economic power and even then, if the State bureaucracy survives, it may be introduced at a level of law but not in
real life. Mindless exponential expansion and ecological
deterioration cannot be stopped with the present structure of
economic and political power. Institutional changes are shallow and short-lived without a revolutionary reorientation of
education. On the other hand, any efforts to create better men
only by means of a series of educational reforms are doomed to
failure without appropriate institutional transformations. Isolated, piecemeal reforms using a method of trial and error will
not do. The restructuring of the whole society is necessary.
Partial reforms could then make sense as steps or phases of an
overall transformation.

## 4   Methods of social change compatible with the prin-
ciple of equal self-determination

In a world that suffers from so many limitations, which is
dominated by so many and such powerful forces, the degree of
self-determination of most people is low. One cannot reasonably expect a *fiat* that would turn them all into active fighters
for their liberation. It is inconceivable, however, that all
humankind will simultaneously stand up on its feet and get rid
of its shackles. It is even less thinkable that after achieving
'negative' freedom, all people will be equally able to create
social institutions that provide optimal conditions for everybody's 'positive' freedom.

Obviously, it is always minorities that start the struggle for
liberation as in all other emancipatory processes worth historical memory. What the present generation knows better than
any other in history is that after producing the initial steps

towards a promising emancipatory breakthrough, and after winning the support of the majority, a victorious minority tends to establish its own rule and to bring the process to a halt. Another essential lesson that one can learn from twentieth century experience is to watch the character of the activists and of the organisation of the movement for emancipation. It is illusory to expect a course of real emancipation to be promoted by power-hungry, ambitious, arrogant, intolerant, envious, competitive leaders and by hierarchical, authoritarian organisations that insist on strict external discipline and monolithic unity.

There may be situations in which there is not much choice. The amount of built-in, structural violence, of injustice, hunger and corruption may be so unbearable that the only chance to get out of that miserable state is to join or support a violent, authoritarian resistance movement. Nevertheless, one should know in advance what one is doing, what one is risking life for. The achievements will be limited, no matter how remarkable: the overthrow of a downright criminal government; agrarian reform; more bread for workers and peasants; more social security. However, after the initial liberating steps a new oligarchy or autocracy will emerge, with as much probability as there can ever be in human affairs. Occasionally a capitalist may renounce his wealth and an autocrat his power, but the chances are very slim indeed.

The world will still have to wait for the emergence of a really democratic broad movement which has a programme of long-range emancipatory social change, and promises to fulfil it. Such a movement presupposes a level of civil liberties already reached by a democratic revolution in the past. Most recent revolutions took place under much worse conditions, in despotic régimes, led by relatively small clandestine organisations that were pushed into illegality and violence by police terror. A really democratic movement does not involve any fixed hierarchy, although it may have superb organisation and able leaders. What makes an organisation superb is well-kept communication lines, a high level of co-operation, internalisation of basic goals by its members, unity of practical purpose, and conscious autonomous discipline. Leaders in such a movement are not self-appointed but elected for limited intervals from a large number of experienced activists. Their most important quality is the ability to formulate clearly what the movement as a whole vaguely feels should be done. Another important ability of a democratic leader is to mediate skilfully among conflicting views and attitudes within the movement, and to indicate solutions agreeable to all. There is no need for one leader to concentrate in his hands all or most leading functions within the movement such as succinct statement of theoretical foundations and of long-range goals; determination of immediate policies; daily resolution of tactical issues; cadres' policy; control of the implementation of adopted decisions. These and other leading functions should be distributed among several leaders. They would rotate, as a matter of rule, but even within their mandate they would be closely watched and critically examined by the membership rather than worshipped and blindly followed. (The fact is that there are not self-made autocratic leaders – they are invariably the product of veneration and uncritical faith of a naïve, politically illiterate, insecure, patriarchal-minded mass.

Such a democratic emancipatory movement has its theory but not an ideology. Its theory is open to debate, it allows a plurality of alternatives concerning unresolved issues. Nevertheless, solutions of some basic issues will be reached and maintained through dialogue. This free concensus on fundamental issues constitutes the ground of the movement, of its unity of will, in spite of all pluralism of views. Ideological propaganda that imposes a fixed creed as obligatory and unrevisable will be replaced by a process of theoretical education in which force of argument cannot be replaced by force of authority, in which everything remains open to reexamination and critical appraisal and in which there is no need to turn wise, learned, but fallible predecessors into sacrosanct classics.

Such a movement employs existing institutions in order to propagate its goals, to win over the majority, and eventually to gain political power and use it for a structural transformation of the given society. What is meant here by 'structural transformation' is the supersession of the defining characteristics of the old system, such as production for profit, alienated labour, and the bureaucratic, oppressive State. It is structural transformation that makes a social change revolutionary and radically emancipatory, not the use of violence, nor the sudden economic collapse of the old system, nor the overthrow of its government. It follows then, that a continuous series of non-violent, far-reaching reforms may be more revolutionary than a violent substitution of one autocratic régime for another;

The present day Left in some European countries approaches, in some respects, the description of such a democratic revolutionary movement. For many good reasons it has aroused the hopes of democratic socialists all over the world. While it aspires to a greater economic freedom and equality it commits itself to political pluralism, to the rules of parliamentary democracy. And yet it suffers from several serious limitations:

1 Eurocommunism, as well as socialist parties, still clings to the traditional forms of political organisation involving some degree of hierarchy and authoritarian decision-making. It is true that Marchais, Berlinguer and Carillo are more subject to a democratic election procedure than most other communist leaders, but they all tend to assume the role of permanent, professional leaders. Rivalry among leaders and among parties is difficult to avoid. A temporary coalition of parties is far less stable and coherent than a unified movement, no matter how pluralistic on a wide range of specific issues.

2 The French Communist Party insists on the nationalisation of many enterprises and whole branches of industry. But it has no clear stand on the issue of self-government. Surely State-owned and controlled enterprises may at best improve material conditions of the workers but will fail to increase the level of their self-determination.

3 The greatest difficulty inherent in the method of 'revolutionary reformism' is a lasting primacy of tactics over strategy so that original revolutionary long-range goals may fall into oblivion. This is a problem which the Italian Communist Party is already facing. In a society in which the middle class is very strong, a political party with a revolutionary long-range programme has a chance of winning a majority if it keeps silent about its ultimate goals, and publicly emphasises its instrumental, short-range goals, such as the protection of civil rights, greater stability and prosperity, full employment, and an improvement of the living standards of the under-privileged. The danger is that in gaining ground with the middle class, and becoming more acceptable as a partner in

'the historical compromise' it will lose ground with the more militant sections of the working class, intelligentsia, and youth.

Another method is pragmatic: the solution of the most urgent social problems as they arise. A vision of a new future society and of a totality of changes leading to it is missing here. A pragmatist is moderately conservative in his attitude toward the existing social structure: as much as possible should be preserved. In this way one at least avoids heavy risks and unnecessary destruction, but also surrenders the power to create essentially new and more rational social arrangements under more favourable conditions. Thus, optimal possibilities may be entirely wasted. A pragmatist is pushed to moderate change by necessity. An advantage over a rigid doctrinaire and an adamant, irrational conservative is that he remains open to change and recognises the necessity when he feels it in practice. This strategy of social change may (although need not) lead to an increase of equal self-determination.

Much of what has happened in Western Europe appears to follow this 'enlightened' pragmatic line. Changes take place under pressure by introducing some element of compromise between the long-range interests of the oppressors and of the oppressed. One example is *decolonisation*. Keeping order and preserving the old colonial rule in rebellious colonies turned out to be too costly. Releasing control to them not only stopped draining the blood of the metropole but also allowed the establishment of new, mutually useful forms of co-operation. 'Commonwealth' replaced empire.

Another example is the introduction of some limited forms of *workers' participation and co-determination*. For workers it was a first step in a long process of increasing self-determination. For capitalists, it was letting some steam out of a dangerously hot engine; it did not deprive them of their power, yet it increased the morale of the workers, shifting part of the responsibility for unpopular decisions to them and blurring to some extent traditional, clear-cut, purely defensive trade-union class consciousness.

A third example is *job enrichment* and *humanisation of work*. In all projects to restructure work within capitalist firms (less significant as 'Corning Glass', 'Motorola', 'Texas Instruments' in the United States or more important as in Volvo's

Kalmar plant in Sweden, 'Hunstos Fabrikken' in Norway or the 'Bolivar Project' in the Harman automobile mirror factory in Tennessee, United States) a common element in mutually conflicting interests was found. Work became more varied and less controlled, workers gained more opportunities to have a say in decisions that affect their work and life, but at the same time, some interests of the capitalists were better protected: personnel turnover and absenteeism decreased, while productivity increased.

The fourth example is *ecological degradation*. Investment in technology to control and decrease pollution also raises production costs and decreases the competitive power of enterprises and national industries. Concessions to the rising pressure of public opinion are nevertheless being made all the time and, paradoxically, the expansive concern over healthy natural surroundings appears to be stronger in capitalism than in State 'socialism'. The most instructive example is the crucial issue of energy. The capitalist establishment is split into two parties: on the one side are the adamant defenders of the existing arrangements, and in particular the defenders of the interests of the oil, automobile and related industries, who refuse even to face the crisis in all its seriousness and lull themselves into optimistic hopes that there may still be more oil than we believe. On the other side, are the pragmatic defenders of the general, long-range interests of capitalism who see the situation more realistically and who realise the need for adaptation. The latter produce programmes for energy saving and building up alternative energy sources. But switching from one source of energy to another affects only particular branches of industry and not capitalism as a whole. It is much more serious with a systematic long-range reduction of consumption and limitation of growth. Capitalism as we know it stands or falls with exponential material output increase – it is incompatible with a zero growth policy. To a pragmatist if something no longer works without substantial repair, the repair will have to be undertaken without bothering too much whether the repaired thing still falls under its former concept or is now something new. It is conceivable, therefore, that a series of pragmatic reforms, beginning with Roosevelt's 'New Deal' embracing decolonisation, growing social security, participation, humanisation of work, conservation of a healthy, natural environment, and a reduction of material growth eventually generates a mixed society with some capitalist and some socialist features, in which the general level of self-determination will be considerably higher than in either present day capitalism or in State socialism, and which will constitute a far more favourable ground for further and more equitable development of self-determination.

The difference between revolutionary and pragmatic reformism may be summarised as follows: the former is a conscious, radical, critical, thought-inspired process of change, with a view of realising the optimal historical possibility of society as a whole (as a *Gestalt*) and as quickly as possible. The latter is a process of change determined by immediate practical necessity, with a view to solving specific tasks one by one, and to preserving all those institutions which are still able to function successfully. If the principle of self-determination is given a methodological interpretation and is taken as a criterion of evaluation of alternative methods of change, then revolutionary reformism is clearly preferable. At the core of this whole work is a basic humanistic assumption that man may not only make his history but may do so in a conscious, rational, free way under given objective constraints. Pragmatism emphasises that man reflects rather than anticipates and creates reality, that he is conditioned by external necessity rather than a decisive element of it. Clearly, the difference is a matter of emphasis; not a clear-cut dichotomy. A humanistic revolutionary must also carefully analyse the objective, historical situation and establish the limits of the framework of possibilities within which he can act freely.

On the other hand, an enlightened pragmatist has conceptual preferences and when pushed to change, he usually acts in the direction of progress and emancipation. After all, he is also a (more cautious) heir of the Enlightenment and liberalism. He must be clearly distinguished from the conservative who does not believe in any change except retrogressive ones. It would appear that the pragmatist's cautiousness must be an advantage over the revolutionary democrat since it involves fewer risks and less human suffering. (The truth is that it involves fewer risks of impatiently destroying an institution which still has some limited emancipatory function – for example, the bourgeois parliamentary system – and replacing it with institutions which hardly even keep the appearance of being more democratic (e.g. a political system totally controlled by one political party).

On the other hand, pragmatism involves another kind of equally serious risk of tolerating inferior institutions when far more emancipatory institutions are at hand (e.g. favouring representative over participatory democracy). The truth is also that pragmatism avoids all that human suffering which goes together with any profound reshaping of society, even when it is not violently executed. On the other hand, pragmatic reformism tolerates for too long a tremendous amount of human suffering which is the result of systematic, built-in injustice and coercion. This may continue throughout the long period while the system is still able to function regardless of unbearable human misery and agony.

A third method of social change is violent revolution. There are situations in which this method is feasible and the only possible one. It is feasible when in an obviously unjust, oppressive, decayed society the centre of power is weak, unstable, corrupt, has little public support and relies on a demoralised army. This method is the only possible way of change when the centre of power is extremely repressive, inflexible, incapable of developing economic, political, and cultural forces in the country, and unwilling to make any concessions and to introduce any reforms. The Third World is full of totally parasitic ruling élites which have nothing in common with the dynamic, entrepreneurial bourgeoisie of eighteenth-and-nineteenth-century Western Europe and America. Instead of engineering full development of the productive capacities of their societies, instead of developing liberal political institutions, education and culture, these élites serve the interests of foreign super powers, sell out domestic natural resources and pile up their private fortunes. Under such conditions, sooner or later, a radical liberation movement emerges that opposes by arms and tries to seize political power. Under those conditions there is little choice but to eliminate vicious, oppressive force by force. The amount of structural violence inherent in the system may be far greater than the amount of direct physical violence needed to realise the change.

This analysis presupposes that a strategy of violent resolution is either not possible or not necessary in some other types of the situation. It is not possible when the centre of power is stable, enjoying considerable popular support and having at its disposal a strong and loyal military force. It is not necessary if, with a strong popular pressure, the government can be pushed into a series of reforms which might achieve more than an incomplete violent revolution.

There are several factors that may prevent reaching the emancipatory objectives of a violent revolution. Such a revolution will be abortive when the use of violence provokes such insecurity, fear and hatred among the middle classes as to trigger a mass shift toward the extreme Right.

It invariably remains incomplete since the use of violence as a means to seize political power requires a type of political organisation (clandestine, centralistic, authoritarian) that has a narrow political horizon and, in case of victory, tends to be transformed into a bureaucratic élite and to freeze revolutionary processes at a relatively early stage. The point is that this may (although need not necessarily) be the only means to overcome stagnation and decay and to make some indispensable steps on the road toward greater freedom and social justice. The Russian, Chinese, Yugoslav and Cuban revolutions have all been incomplete, but to various degrees they produced social structures which are, historically considered, a more favourable take-off ground for further emancipation than the previous corrupt, decaying régimes.

From there further development may proceed in several possible ways. The official ideology tells that a classless, stateless, marketless, communist society would inevitably emerge as the result of scientific and technological revolution. It is not apparent, though, how any amount of mechanisation, computerisation and material well-being alone help get rid of ruling bureaucracy and increase the level of self-determination.

The view of some dissidents and libertarian socialists is that sooner or later the working class will organise a new violent anti-bureaucratic revolution. It does not require a great deal of knowledge and wisdom to come to the conclusion that the task of organising such a rebellion is hardly feasible. It can easily be suppressed in its initial stages since the coercive organs of the State are stronger, better equipped, and better supported by a vast network of informers than in any other society in history. And if an organised, illegal opposition manages to seize power, all counter-revolutionary forces outside and inside the country will join and try to use the movement for their own purposes. Having again a narrowly political character, to win power, such an anti-bureaucratic movement would, in the unlikely case of victory, reproduce another bureaucratic élite.

Another alternative is pragmatic adaptation to necessities under the pressure of a powerful emancipatory public opinion. Once a State 'socialist' society is industrialised and inevitably, in spite of all artificial barriers, joins the ranks of other developed countries, it will too become exposed (on a quickly increasing mass scale) to modern emancipatory demands: for participation, workers' control, civil rights, ethnic autonomy, free international travel and communication, modern arts, universalisation of culture, new forms of communal life of youth, women's liberation. A growing dissatisfaction with the restrictions of the system and the unnecessary austerity of life-style will irresistably push toward democratisation and the relaxation of the ideological grip. This is a very slow process, but obviously present after the death of great charismatic leaders – Stalin in Russia in 1953, and Mao in China in 1976.

Emancipation through pragmatic readjustments to the overwhelming demands of the time is neither inevitable nor very fast in either highly developed capitalism or in 'real socialism'. But – in the absence of a powerful, universal, democratic socialist movement – it may be the only real alternative to stagnation and barbarism.

## 5 Revolutionary reformism and class domination

Revolutionary reformism claims that a discontinuous structural change of the whole society need not be a matter of sudden collapse and destruction of the old system followed by a rapid building of a new system, but may be constituted by a series of partial changes which individually appear as continuous but, as a whole, abolish some basic limitations of the old society and gradually clear the ground for the building of the new one.

This claim may be challenged on the ground that no amount of reforms can do away with the class domination of the old society, and that the abolition of class domination must be one, single, discontinuous act such as abolition of private property.

The element of truth here is that transcendence of class domination is indispensable for any new society based on equal self-determination. But in order to see what this transcendence involves, and whether it is a simple discontinuous act or a discontinuity comprising a series of continuous steps, the concept of class and class domination must be analysed.

Among those who analyse society in terms of its class structure there should be no serious controversy about the following explication of the concept of class.

A *class* is a broad group of people within a given society who share a similar social position, and common economic and political interests.

The following four features determine the *social position*: 1) ownership status of the means of production; 2) the role in the production process; 3) participation in social decision-making, in particular in economic and political management; and 4) the nature of income, and the part taken in the distribution of surplus product.

1) Ownership of the means of production is not a simple property; it can be analysed into at least four different powers related to given means of production which often (but not necessarily ) go together:

a) the power to dispose autonomously of the means of production; b) the power to appropriate the large share of the surplus value produced by the use of the means of production (by surplus value is meant the difference between the value of produced goods and the invested capital); c) the power to alienate (to sell, give away); and d) the power to bequeath.

In all societies divided into classes, there is a group of individuals who do not possess any means of production (the proletariat): a group of small owners (the middle class – farmers, artisans, shopkeepers, co-operativists, and small stockholders); and a group of big owners (landowners, and industrialists).

Already a static class analysis, before we even consider what happens with private property during a process of social change, shows that some of these four property powers may combine to the exclusion of some others. For example, top political functionaries in a State-owned and controlled economy have the power to dispose fully of the national means of production as if they owned them. They can also appropriate a part of the surplus value in the form of large material privileges; but they have no rights to alienate and to bequeath State property to their relatives.

2) From the point of view of the role performed in socially necessary work, the division is again quite clear: there is, at one extreme, a social group responsible for all mechanical, alienating, manual work, and at the other, a group which has the privilege of being engaged in the intellectual operations of organising, investigating, administering, planning, and creating new institutions and enterprises. Between these two, but closer to the manual workers, there is a group engaged either in repetitive and mechanical intellectual work, or in highly skilled, and yet alienating, manual work.

3) In most societies workers do not participate in any kind of economic or social decision-making; they are entirely powerless and excluded from society. All power to take basic policy decisions is in the hands of top executives, major stockholders, and leading political functionaries. The middle class has a limited power in the micro-structure of social organisation, in the departments of big enterprises, in local communities and local political organisations, and in independent small enterprises.

4) The nature and source of income is a very good indicator of class-identity – that is why Marx took it for the starting point of his incomplete analysis of classes (in the last, 52nd, chapter of the third volume of *Capital*). The workers' source of income are wages – the amount necessary to maintain and reproduce employed labour force. Upper classes live either on land rent (big landowners) or on surplus value, which they distribute among themselves in different forms and shares. Capitalists appropriate the lion's share in the form of profit; technocrats get a part of it in the form of very high salaries which greatly exceed the appropriate compensation for work itself, no matter how highly skilled or creative. In addition to salaries, professional political functionaries enjoy various, more or less concealed, material privileges ('fringe benefits').

A contradictory position is characteristic of the middle classes; those who belong to this class either live on the products of their own work (small owners, farmers, artisans), sharing thus the destiny of both producers and owners of the means of production, or they function in both roles of an exploited wage-earner, and of a small stockholder, who adds to his small income the surplus value appropriated from another producer.

Although these four criteria applied separately do not yield identical class divisions, and in each case there is some overlapping, it follows from the preceding analysis that one can reasonably clearly distinguish three large groupings:

1) *The working class* embraces not only direct producers in industry, but also hired workers in agriculture, workers in the services, and many intellectual workers. Here belong all those who are deprived of all ownership powers, of any real power to influence social decision-making processes, all those who are compelled to perform according to the necessity of the technological process or of the strictly heteronomously determined rules, and who live exclusively on compensation for their work, without taking any part in the distribution of surplus value.

2) *Upper classes*: capitalists, big landowners, top managers, the ruling political élite who enjoy property rights, have a monopoly of economic and political power, are free from manual work and distribute among themselves appropriated surplus value.

3) *Middle classes*: small owners, small stockholders, technicians, low functionaries who have a contradictory social position because they share some properties with the working class and some with the upper classes.

Such clear differences in social positions are reflected in the sharp opposition of respective common interests. As the concept of interest suggests, it involves an *objective* and a *subjective* dimension. The former derives from the objective situation of a group in a historical situation, and from the real possibility to change that position. The latter is the awareness of an interest which does not only depend on objective position, but also on various empirical factors (such as the force of tradition, the impact of the official ideology, foreign political conflicts, etc.).

In spite of all variability of empirical (subjective) working-class interests from place to place, an objective, common interest of the working class is to overcome material misery and spiritual pauperism; to abolish unemployment; to reduce the level of exploitation – and eventually to do away with it altogether; to improve working conditions, increase safety, and reduce working hours in correlation to the increase of productivity of work.

The interests of the various factions of the ruling class hardly ever fully coincide, and in some situations may even be in conflict. Capitalists are naturally mostly interested in the maximisation of profit, technocrats in growth and efficiency, political bureaucracy in the maximal authority of existing institutions. (These may be mutually exclusive under certain conditions.) But these factions tend to be unified against the labour movement and any other social force that disturbs the balance of the system and challenges its basic institutions. Their interest is in defending 'law and order', in preserving social structure as it is, and in achieving a satisfactory rate of growth and of profit increase.

The interests of the middle class are as contradictory as its social position. It may oppose exploitation and oppression built in the system but it also fears the destruction of that system and consequent loss of its property. In a situation of a profound crisis it may play both revolutionary and reactionary roles. The vacillation of French middle classes 1968–1981 is a good example.

The concept of *class domination* is implicit in the proposed analysis of the class structure in modern societies.

The relation between two social groups is a relation of domination if 1) one group can survive only by selling a substantial part of its existence – of its time and energy – to the other; 2) one group is pushed into dehumanising drudgery while all organising and directing activity remain in the hands of the other; 3) one group has the monopoly on all decision-making; 4) one group accumulates a disproportionate part of social wealth by having control over the other group's products.

The whole point of this analysis is to show that the dominated class may liberate in a number of steps, and not just in one big jump that at once removes all aspects of class domination.

1) Misleading terminology sometimes suggests discontinuity where the process cannot but be continuous. For

example, the expression 'abolition of private property' suggests that one can, by one decree, both do away with all private ownership and socialise the means of production. As a matter of fact that has never happened. Socialisation was confused with 'nationalisation', where private ownership is transformed into State ownership, and where the State bureaucracy still retains some essential property functions. But even 'nationalisation' of the whole economy is hardly feasible – it usually involves several phases, beginning with key enterprises and banks, proceeding towards smaller ones. And even where nationalisation takes place, an element of continuity preserves the economy from disruption and collapse. Chinese revolutionaries gave former capitalists managerial functions and partly refunded nationalised property. Unlike Russian Bolsheviks, they were able to benefit considerably from the loyalty and skills of their former class enemy.

The process of socialisation of the means of production definitely begins within capitalist society wherever Left liberals (like Roosevelt) or trade unions (like the British Labour party or Swedish Social Democrats) came to power. None of the four mentioned property powers remained the same as in early classical capitalism. The State encroachments upon private property rights are increasingly significant. Whole branches have been nationalised. In those which have not, private owners dispose of their means within the framework of State legal regulations, and State financial and economic policies. They share with the State the surplus value. In some countries taxation is effectively progressive, and most profit is used for extended reproduction, and not for private consumption. This kind of profit already has a contradictory character and undergoes a process of change. Its egoistic, wasteful dimension is related to the capitalists' private consumption which has now reached its limits. The other greater part of profit that is re-invested has an aspect which is compatible with social interests: it contributes to development, the results of which escape the control of the capitalist within the given social framework. Another aspect of that part of profit is anti-social: the more invested capital, the more social power in the hands of indivdiuals. But we shall see later that a process is underway that already tends to reduce the sheer power of holding stock.

Another property power – to bequeath one's wealth to posterity – has also been somewhat modified. Inheritance tax is increased. Ageing individuals who accumulated a fortune will have to choose between either formally bequeathing it to individual inheritors but actually transferring most of it anonymously into State property, or transferring it into socialised property associated with their name in the form of a foundation or an endowment.

Finally, selling property may turn into a process of eliminating private property, of its transformation into State property. What is missing is a simple law, easily conceivable in State capitalism, saying that (in the national interest) no private property of a specified kind can be sold without first being offered to the State.

2) Within capitalism the original, sharp dichotomy is already blurred between the sheer drudgery of the worker – brought to its extreme in the assembly-line – and the imaginative organising work of the entrepreneur. Early union of property and entrepreneurship was split, and on the one side emerged the owner without function, on the other the functioning manager without property. The existence of the former became parasitic; the latter, being essentially a salaried employee, became transferrable to post-capitalist society. Automated technology somewhat reduced alienation and offered both more freedom from the rhythm of machinery and more opportunity for communication and problem-solving.

3) In the decision-making process, too, the situation is not as simple as it was at the time of *laissez-faire* capitalism when the demarcation line was quite sharp between totally powerless workers and omnipotent employers. In recent decades there has been a steady increase of workers' participation and co-determination, although still only in less crucial matters and without decisive influence. On the other hand, most owners' earlier power has vanished. A major part of it went into the hands of technocracy, and a good deal of it was appropriated by State bureaucracy. The latter lays down some policy constraints within which the former actually runs the enterprises. The stockholders, represented by a board of directors, retain overall control, the power to hire and fire the management and to secure a satisfactory level of profits.

4) Finally, the distribution of surplus value is a far more complex affair nowadays than in the early days of capitalism. Organised labour gets back a part in the form of social security and substantial wage increases. The State and technocracy get the lion's share; and most of what remains, in the form of net profit, is reinvested.

All these changes took place within capitalism. The crucial question, however, is whether it is, in principle, possible, and at what point, to go beyond the boundaries of capitalism. Only then would it make sense to make a distinction between ordinary, conformist reformism and the *revolutionary reformism*.

Capitalism is transcended when wealth stops being capital, that is when it no longer generates profit and social power. This happens under two conditions:

1) when the return for an investment is no longer profit but a fixed interest (comparable to what any bank in any socialist country pays to a citizen who postpones consumption of his share of the product of associated past labour for some future purpose); 2) when investment into the means of production does not yield any managment rights (in other words, when the stockholders, board of directors, or the corresponding supervising State agency, are replaced by a self-governing council democratically elected by all employees of the enterprise).

Any Labour party in power (and for a long time this has been a reality in England and Northern Europe), any socialist coalition government (which is a real possibility in some southern European countries) could realise both conditions. The policy inspired by this kind of social change is hardly likely to produce more resistance than 'nationalisation'. Nationalisation breaks any link between the former owner and the enterprise. Therefore, it appears to be radical and revolutionary; in reality it may only be a step from private capitalism to State capitalism. From the point of view of the worker the change may be totally insignificant and hardly perceptible: a change of employer, and the continuation of hired, alienated work, without any say in the management process. It could be worse – less freedom to strike and a struggle for the improvement of working conditions. The fulfilment of these two conditions is much more radical than it appears to be. The former owner now becomes a creditor; his capital is transformed into a loan. If he has any special skills and expertise, the enterprise might need them. And yet, socially, the break is truly revolutionary. The power of the capitalist is over, the relation between him and the workers will no longer be a relation of exploitation, no more than the relation between the citizen of a socialist country who buys bonds for building a railway (and gets some interest for them) and the workers of the railway. The road to bureaucratisation is precluded due to the introduction of self-management; in comparison to nationalisation, the only big loser is State bureaucracy. And the great winner is the workers' collective in the enterprise, which now gets all the policy-making power.

This redistribution of power in the economy may involve as many steps as is necessary and feasible. When the process is over, a society emerges which is still mixed, but in which there is no longer any dominating class. The basic contradiction in this new society is between the principle of equal self-determination materialised in the new self-managing councils (in the whole social micro-structure) and the principle of external heteronomous determination materialised in the still existing apparatus of the State (which dominates social macro-structure and pushes hard to dominate self-managing bodies themselves).

This contradiction may be resolved 1) by the establishment of the full hegemony of the State, and the reduction of workers' councils to a mere ideological façade; 2) by stagnation and decay; and 3) by the transformation of the organs of the State into organs of self-government, by the affirmation of the principle of equal self-determination in the whole society in economy, politics and culture at the micro- and macro-level.

# 4 Decentralisation – A Precondition of a More Rational Society

The concept of rationality that has dominated Western culture and social life since the seventeenth century involved a belief in large, centrally-controlled systems. Since Descartes, Spinoza, Leibniz and Newton the ideal of science and philosophy has been the systematisation of all knowledge and its exact derivation from a minimum number of central principles. The ideal of political organisation, exemplified in absolute monarchies, philosophically expressed in Hobbes and Hegel, revived in new forms after dramatic twentieth century upheavals (the great Depression in the West, incomplete socialist revolutions in the East) has been an excessively centralised State which, in the name of security, reason and justice, takes care of an established social order. Analogously, there is a steady trend towards increasing centralisation in Western economy – from small workshops to ever bigger enterprises, then to monopolies, increasing State control, and eventually to huge multi-national corporations and multi-State economic communities.

From the point of view of the ultimate purpose of this specifically Western concept of rationality – unlimited increase of human efficiency, increase of power and of wealth – centralism was quite successful. Another important ingredient of Western culture – the idea of human freedom – had to retreat constantly. At each new step toward centralisation, resistance was offered in the name of freedom, but invariably in vain. Manufacture had no chance against the assembly-line and automation; *laissez-faire* had to give way to State capitalism, federation to quickly growing bureaucratic leviathans, small provincial towns to huge overcrowded cities, self-produced, local culture to uniform mass media culture.

To be sure, not all that was small, loose and autonomous deserved to survive, nor is its disappearance to be regretted. There was never so much exploitation as in the days of *laissez-faire* and fully 'free competition'. Behind the facade of autonomy and self-determination of federal units, most drastic forms of racism, political and religious intolerance, and oppression of unprotected minorities may take place. Small masters are not necessarily more merciful than big ones.

And yet the whole traditional bourgeois concept of rationality, with its identification of progress with unlimited growth and increasing efficiency within big centralised systems, is now in profound crisis.

A point has been reached when further exponential growth on a planet with limited natural resources threatens to destroy irreversibly the natural environment. The degree of alienation of work in centralised technological systems has become unbearable and begins to constitute a barrier to any further increase in productivity. Concentration of corporate and State power meets stronger resistance than ever in the form of mass demands for participation and reduction of excessive bureaucratic machinery.

The very ground of rationality on which modern centralism rests has now become problematic. If reason is used only to increase efficiency and power this is purely instrumental rationality, since these cannot be the ultimate purposes of human life. Efficiency is obviously a means which can be used for both oppressive and emancipatory purposes. And power can be both creative power but also power to dominate others.

## 1 Basic limitations of centralism

Centralism is one of the most characteristic features of this rationality of efficiency and domination. However, in the same way in which rationality of domination can be challenged from an irrational standpoint, as well as from the point of view of a rationality of emancipation, a critique of centralism can be both an expression of naïve, romantic refusal for any growth and of nostalgia for traditional, pre-capitalist forms of life, as well as a thoughtful, radically new project of overcoming the basic limitations of centralised patterns of social life. The former regards centralism as merely an evil, pathological phenomenon and overlooks the fact that there were strong reasons for its emergence, and that, under conditions of accelerated social growth, it met urgent needs for order and for indispensable co-ordination in an increasingly more complex society. A more adequate critique recognises those useful historical functions of centralism but finds it deficient today for both philosophical and practical reasons. It focuses on its following essential limitations:

1) Each centralised system has a hierarchical structure. Power is concentrated at the centre and transferred towards the periphery. The whole society is divided into layers such that one closer to the periphery is subordinated to one closer to the centre. Whatever the form of legitimation of central authority, this hierarchical structure involves a tremendous amount of domination. This is not hidden in all those systems where central authority is ascribed divine origin. The purpose of modern political ideologies is to conceal this fact. The social contract theory postulates a fictitious delegation of power from individual citizens to a central political authority. Citizens are denied the right to return their power – which would be a permanent possibility if they were not dominated, and if they ever really delegated power voluntarily. Another political ideology of our time tends to justify the central authority by ascribing its bearer the status of a revolutionary, history-making vanguard of the vast majority of the population. But unless the vanguard is given the free consent of that population, it is no more than a self-appointed master. So-called 'democratic centralism' has nothing democratic in it: a well-organised élite, holding firmly all levers of power, will never fail to secure a majority. The only difference is that while in some systems minorities are guaranteed the right to continue to defend their particular views, in democratic centralism they are compelled to conform fully.

2) What follows from hierarchy of power is a high degree of heteronomy. An element of heteronomy is inevitable in every complex society, no matter how genuinely democratic. Certain common issues will have to be solved for the society as a whole. If this is done in a democratic way, particular communities will elect their representatives and these will reach a solution as a result of dialogue and eventual consensus. Such a solution will often be the result of a compromise and will contain undesired elements. The amount of heteronomy increases enormously in a centralistic system for at least three reasons. First, there are too many issues decided at the level of

global society, although they are of such a nature that they do not necessarily require a high level of co-ordination, and could therefore be regulated by local and regional communities themselves. Second, the representatives are no longer fully responsible to the electorate in their communities – they are also dependent on and responsible to the central State apparatus, central party and centres of corporate power. Third, once there is a strong central authority it has all kinds of ways of interfering with an apparently democratic decision-making process.

3) The more centralised a system the more mediation is needed between the centre of power and the people. A special social group is needed to play this mediating role: bureaucracy. There are some differences between a liberal bureaucracy which treats all citizens as interchangeable and therefore insists on the strict application of the rules (Weberian bureaucracy), and a totalitarian bureaucracy which assumes a stratified concept of citizenship – so that some individuals are regarded above the law and others below it. In both cases, however, the sacred principle of any bureaucracy is order; by its very existence it kills all initiative and spontaneity except from the centre. Keeping the existing established order by all means and against any 'pathological' deviation, disturbance and unrest, constitutes the particular interest of bureaucracy and of the centre it serves. This particular interest is invariably construed as the general social interest; no centralised system can survive without some kind of mystifying ideology. While one of the functions of ideology is to legitimate dominating power, the other is to conceal existing forms of exploitation. Thus the image of bureaucracy is created and maintained as of a precious social force, in the absence of which society would fall apart, and which deserves excessive salaries and privileges for its expertise. The truth is, of course, that basic decision-making in general, and creative, innovative co-ordination in particular, require far more wisdom and understanding than bureaucratic expertise, and that to the extent to which the special skills and techniques are indispensable they need not go together with any dominating power.

4) While claiming rationality and efficiency, all centralised systems suffer from a specific form of inefficiency and waste. Decisions are taken at a considerable distance from the place of

action and they are too often made after an adverse delay. It is true the distance allows an overview, so that the problem is seen in the context of the whole system, and, other conditions being equal, a holistic appoach to a particular issue is more rational than an atomistic one. But other conditions are not equal, nor is atomism the only alternative to an abstract holism that characterises bureaucratic ways of thinking. Other conditions are not equal since being on the spot allows richer, more reliable, first-hand information, and since many public issues are of such local importance, that they need not be regulated from a distance. At which level of social organisation – local, regional or global – a public issue should be regulated is a problem that cannot be solved by a general formula. In each case a number of factors has to be considered. Whatever apparent gains from uniformity and inter-relatedness within a big system, the losses may be overwhelming. One would have to operate on the basis of scanty, abstract, reifying information, missing too many psychological factors, lacking real understanding of the specific situation. The centre invariably tends to impose simple, uniform, elegant-looking solutions for the whole system. But complex, irregular-looking solutions may do much better justice to diversity of the various parts within the system. Worst of all, human beings feel responsible in proportion to the freedom they have to contribute by their own autonomous actions to a given course of events. The more often they have to wait for orders from the centre, the less responsible they feel, and the more passive, apathetic, and alienated they become. When this happens, individuals and groups stop caring about the public good, no one takes the initiative in cases where the public interest is at stake, and things drag on in a routine way with far too little initiative to introduce the necessary innovations. In that sense all centralised systems tend to become barriers to qualitative development no matter how much they may foster quantitative growth.

Herein lies the root of the present-day crisis of centralism. It was instrumental to expansion, domination and conquest. But the point has been reached when even the most advanced countries can no longer solve their problems by mindless expansion and exploitation of natural and human resources. Changing nature beyond certain boundaries turns out to be changing the only natural conditions under which human survival is at all possible. Domination breeds hatred and rebellion sooner or later; instead of continuing to expand, centuries old dominating powers have now been compelled to retreat and lose ground. Once it is no longer possible to plunder the riches of the whole world and to build an illusory prosperity at the expense of the misery of the whole of humankind, an incurable internal sickness develops and all impressive efficiency begins to turn into a horrifying wastefulness. But if, after all, saving, modesty, frugality, reduction of excessive material needs are indispensable, then the whole system which claimed the very opposite values has become redundant.

## 2 The philosophical ground of decentralisation

Extreme forms of centralism – fascist or Stalinist totalitarianism – presuppose complete subordination of the individual to some kind of abstract, collective entity. In the case of fascism man is a mere element of the State, nation or race; his unique personality has to give way fully to the unity of all those with whom he shares blood, territory and aggressive goals, expressed by a superhuman leader. In the case of Stalinism, man is predominantly a class-being and tends to subordinate individual aspirations to objective class interests, which sometimes may be known scientifically and are again best expressed by a superwise leader. From both of these views any tendency toward decentralisation would jeopardise the unity of the nation, State, or movement, of the Party. Here is a striking similarity between ideologies which otherwise have very different historical functions, and start from different premises about social structure: one assumes unity of classes, the other class struggle; one tends to preserve economic inequalities of the bourgeois society, the other seeks to abolish them partially at least. What makes them excessively centralised is that whatever their goals, they tend to achieve them in an extremely authoritarian and violent way.

It might seem then, that the only alternative is individualism, the view that each man is unique and is justified in pursuing his own, private, freely chosen aims and interests. However, as liberal political philosophy anticipates, and ample historical experience convincingly shows, extreme individualism, if coherent, cannot be lived; and if incoherent, leads increasingly to unpleasant forms of centralism. It cannot be lived since pursuit of exclusively private egoistic aims produces a state of permanent warfare and utter insecurity. On the other hand, once a special social force is established to provide over-all security and keep order, it may again become increasingly centralised. That liberalism is not immune from centralism has always been evident in France, and has recently become obvious in almost every liberal State.

Far from being a real alternative to totalitarianism, egoistic individualism, with its glaring social inequalities and feeble sense of social integrity, often paves the way to it. What all those ideologies have in common is the denial that human beings have an inherent capacity to understand what social needs are and what would be the rational way to meet them. Man is in fact both a unique person *and* a social being. As an individual he has a distinctive, creative potential and develops quite specific needs and aspirations. But the new-born biological organism becomes a human being only in a society – learning a language, a logic, a morality, acquiring cultural heritage of the whole mankind. He belongs to a family, a nation, a class but also shares certain capacities and needs with all other human beings. He needs personal freedom. Hitlers and Stalins may deprive him of it by brutal force but only temporarily. Where all advocates of egoistic individualism (e.g. Stirner) are wrong is in confusing personal freedom with unlimited egoism. The human need to be free goes together with another essential need – to be recognised and esteemed in the community to which one belongs. Self-realisation has an inner limit in a concern about the well-being of others; in that sense human freedom is responsible. Far from being a normal human condition, egoistic, irresponsible behaviour may always be shown to be the consequence of bad, negligent, abusive treatment in the early stages of one's growth. But, if egoism, acquisitiveness and aggression are not inevitable, genetically-determined traits of human nature, but patterns produced by education, than any political philosophy based on the assumption of egoistic human nature no longer holds ground.

The only philosophical basis for a genuine alternative to

centralism is the conception of man as a being capable of solving at least some social issues in a rational and responsible way. Neither is it assumed here that all individuals have equal problem-solving capacities, nor that all problems can be directly resolved in elementary living and working communities. There are specially gifted individuals, and there are very complex problems common to a whole country, group of countries, or the world at large. One should also distinguish political and technical dimensions of problem-solving. The point here is that each individual is able to participate in political decision-making at least at the elementary level of social organisation. This is exactly what each form of centralism denies. Both moderate liberalist and extreme totalitarian centralism share the view that the ordinary citizen lacks the competence for efficient decision-making and whatever his rights and opportunities to influence the central political authority, the authority itself must stay in the hands of a professional, political élite for an unlimited period. The alleged incompetence of citizens in one case derives from selfishness, in another from unawareness of objective class interest, and in the third from the lack of insight which only great leaders may have. Further, the degree to which citizens are deprived of political power is significantly different: in liberalism they are at least free to vote and to express critical views; in totalitarianism they are only free to follow. The professional political élite is formed in different ways, and it may be more or less open to newcomers. And yet what every centralism presupposes is that its *locus* is a political sphere, and that the whole society is divided into a small group of professional political *subjects* and a large mass of more or less passive, irresponsible political *objects*.

The basic philosophical argument of those who oppose any centralism may be summarised in the following way: since political dimensions of social decision-making require reason, responsibility, personal integrity, wisdom and understanding of social needs – and these are general capacities of all human individuals rather than special technical skills – there is no need for any concentration of power in the hands of professional politicians. Problems will be solved where they arise, at the lowest possible level of social organisation, by all concerned citizens or their responsible non-professional representatives.

## 3   Particular communities and global society – the idea of federalism

So far we have discussed the relationship of the individual citizen and society. Since the society has a multi-level structure and problems arise at different levels, it is necessary to consider the relation of basic communities and higher level communities – eventually the global society.

From the point of view of simple analytical thinking, that projects clear-cut dichotomies into each conceptual framework, it seems that we have to choose between the integrity of the whole and its disintegration into component parts. In the first case local and regional communities are subordinated to the global society. Within it there is a unity of laws, unity of policies and a unique sense of direction imposed by a centre of power. This is the case of centralism. Since the price which has to be paid for the unity of the global system is a considerable loss of freedom of the parts, disintegrative forces may become so strong that the whole falls apart. Now its former components enjoy the benefits of autonomy but suffer from the lack of co-ordination. Moreover, the status of the minorities within the parts may deteriorate once they lose legal protection from the former centralised order.

A real alternative to both is *federalism*. This term is used here in the most general sense of a union of any kinds of community (national States, provinces, cultural or political organisations etc.) which collaborate as equal partners, while preserving a high degree of autonomy. A federation of this kind is possible when all component communities have an objective interest in co-operation, in sharing certain natural or cultural resources, in exchanging goods and experiences, in joining efforts against natural forces or some other common threat. Thus the basic assumption of the federation is that it is a free creation of the parts, rather than a primary whole that determines the conditions of its parts. No matter how high a degree of co-ordination in a union of this type, it does not have any dominating centre, because none of its component units aspire to domination and/or because all of them strongly resist any such tendency. The stability of such a federation depends on a balance of two opposed forces. One works irreversibly toward greater identity and uniformity, the other maintains diversity and preserves specific communal traditions and cultural values. In the same way in which an individual experiences a community as an indispensable social environment when he acts freely and develops in it, a community willingly accepts a larger society as its natural surroundings when it can freely develop within it, autonomously decide on its specific problems, equally participate in the solution of issues common to the whole society and when it can collaborate with other parts without being abused or exploited by any of them. In fact the level of co-ordination among parts can be higher in a federation than in a centralised system. What makes it a federation is equal distribution of power regardless of size, and full political, economic and cultural self-determination.

While conceptual clarity is essential for building clear, transparent relations within any large association, experience with existing federations indicates all kinds of difficulties requiring sometimes rather ingenious solutions.

One such difficulty is difference in size and population. If ordinary democratic rules are applied, a bigger and more populous federal unit will have a larger electorate, a bigger number of representatives in the federal self-governing body (federal assembly) and consequently more power. Purely quantitative and representative democracy must be adjusted to diminish the importance of numbers, and to protect the interests of minorities. But if this is done, following John Stuart Mill, by giving more weight to some votes than to others, this destroys the equality of the individual citizen, and may damage the bigger units. Such a difficult problem can only partly be solved by building a more sophisticated institutional arrangement. For example:

1) The federal assembly would consist of several chambers. In one all federal units would be represented by an equal number of representatives, regardless of the size and population of the unit. Such a chamber would separately discuss and vote, with a right of veto, on all those issues that are vital to the interests of any particular federal unit. A second chamber would be composed of the representatives of all individual citizens – since a federation is ultimately an association of people, and not of abstract entities, and many issues will be common or cut across other than particular federal units' interests.

2) Conflicts of interest among two groups, or between one group and the rest cannot be resolved by a simple vote. The only method at the disposal is dialogue, negotiation and eventually consensus. All kinds of objections are possible here. The method may be too slow in a situation that requires prompt solutions. The compromise reached after all parties make concessions, need not be the most rational one. Negotiations do not take place under the public eye, and individuals who take part seem to acquire some special powers; thus this procedure does not even impress one as being too democratic. Then what about efficiency? Where is the guarantee that such agreements would really be implemented?

Surely this, in the short run, need not be the most efficient or instrumentally rational way of conflict resolution. Those for whom efficiency and instrumental rationality are supreme values may opt for centralism. This method is optimal for those who commit themselves to autonomy and equal distribution of power. A price has to be paid for each choice. A federal society may deliberately decide to invest in development of full self-determination of all its constitutive communities. In the long run it is more rational and may be even more efficient: too impatient and careless handling of initial tensions might later result in explosive and irreparable cleavages.

However the survival of a stable, harmonious federation cannot be secured only by more complex institutional arrangements and more democratic methods of conflict resolution. There must be a political culture that combines autonomy with solidarity, genuine pluralism with a universal emancipatory rationality. Pluralism is indispensable to understand and respect the different needs of others. Yet, whoever requests understanding for his particular needs when they conflict with the needs of others must be able to rationally justify them. An association would fall apart if its constituent communities only pursued their selfish particular interests, fought all the time, and squeezed out half-satisfactory compromise solutions. The purpose of a common political culture, the part of which must be explicitly expressed in the constitution, is to provide a consensus in basic premises of any conflict resolution. Such basic premises are first, agreement as to ultimate preferences, other conditions being equal; second, agreement as to which ultimate preferences have priority when other conditions are not equal, and when they happen to be mutually incompatible. When a federal unit, for selfish reasons, raises a particular issue, it will be invited to justify it with reference to generally accepted principles. Dialogues cannot be won with short-sighted, self-centred policies. It is true, these policies can be stubbornly defended once one escapes the field of rational and moral discourse and turns to formalistic legal rationalisation. After all, it is conceivable that, using its veto power, a part may blackmail the rest of the society. But in such a case either the particular discordant leadership would lose the support of its own constituency and would be recalled, or the federation's social fabric would collapse and it would fall apart.

Another essential difficulty of federalism is a gap in the level of economic and cultural development of various parts. It is hardly possible to achieve full autonomy and equal distribution of power when some parts are much less developed than the others. It is conceivable that, while commodity production still exists, a loose federal structure may even allow an increase of the gap. Centralism may be more efficient in closing it, but at the expense of strengthening a lasting, alienated authoritarian power. Since federalism by its very nature excludes the use of authoritarian central force, it may resort only to those means which are compatible with the autonomy and self-determination of each unit. Such is solidarity. One of the basic purposes of living in any community is mutual aid, support of the whole to any of its parts when coping with a problem that exceeds its own powers. It is important to note here that while 'aid' appears to be a one-way operation – a humanitarian act – it is, in fact, an expression of mutuality, and justice. It is indeed a return to the less developed of what was taken from them in terms of cheap food, raw materials and less expensive labour. On the other hand, aid to overcome backwardness need not be justified on moral grounds alone; it is not only a moral obligation. Under deeper scrutiny it also turns out to be a rational thing, a matter of mutual interest. Growing social inequalities among the parts intensify conflicts and make the federation increasingly vulnerable and unstable. On the other hand, investment into self-development is a much more reasonable and less costly policy than a myriad of welfare programmes with all its waste, bureaucracy and condemnation to passivity. Parts that overcome material misery and begin to approach affluency become much better partners for the exchange of goods and services. Certain issues can be resolved only in a global way; for example, efforts of more developed federal units to improve the quality of the natural environment do not make much sense if the backward ones cannot afford to join them. In a world of growing interdependence federalism appears to be the optimal way of transcending underdevelopment.

## 4  Decentralisation and technological rationality

A great deal of the appeal of centralism has always been derived from its claim that it best meets the demands of efficiency and technological rationality. We have seen that many social activities do not require centralised planning and control in order to run efficiently, and that often regulation from a distance on the basis of scanty and delayed information, following abstract rules, may produce considerable waste and damage. It goes without saying that all such activities should be decentralised as much as possible – which does not exclude an exchange of experiences and spontaneous collaboration.

The problem for federalism is how to deal with certain activities which are a common concern, which require common natural and human resources, a high level of well-ordered co-ordination, with division of roles and unique direction. Such are energy production, public transport, protection of the natural environment, production of indispensable raw materials, and defence. This is where centralism is at its best. Could a decentralised society run those activities nearly efficiently enough?

Two alternative answers are possible to such a question: extreme decentralism, advocated by some traditional anarchists (Godwin, Hodgkins, Warren, Tucker) and some contemporary ecologists, holds that all big systems are intrinsically bad and that all those activities that require them (for example nuclear energy, jet transport, big cities) ought to be abandoned. Giving up a part of power over nature would be a reasonable price to pay for a reduction of authoritarian social power.

Moderate decentralism rejects only those big systems which are inevitably authoritarian such as the State, the political Party, the professional army, the Church, and the business corporation. Those systems which can be regulated in a self-governing, federalist way deserve to be preserved and further developed if they increase productivity, reduce alienated labour and allow a higher level of satisfaction of human needs. Free movement in space, direct acquaintance with other cultures, cultivation of friendships with individuals who belong to other nations, races and civilisations are such needs. They cannot be satisfied without the modern technology of travel which requires complex systems. Energy needs cannot be met without large electricity networks, and fusion nuclear power may be the only energy source to keep human civilisation going when all the fossil fuels have been consumed. Big systems of gathering and conveying information too often serve the established powers, but are not intrinsically authoritarian, and may very efficiently satisfy universal human need for knowledge and liberation from blind natural forces. Ecological problems also belong to those which can be successfully attacked only on a large scale. Whatever an isolated community does against polluted air, water or earth, its efforts are futile without co-ordination with other communities.

To sum up, excessive decentralisation suffers from the following shortcomings:

1) Absence of necessary co-ordination leads to disorder, waste of natural resources, inefficiency.

2) A low level of productivity requires more labour, yet produces more poverty. Many important human needs cannot be met with small-scale technology.

3) Small-scale social organisation and limitation of needs makes many rare, specific human skills redundant. Specialised scientific research, high arts, and top achievements in physical culture cannot be supported by small, self-reliant communities. Hardly any goal can justify a reduction of an already achieved high level of human creativity.

4) The inevitable social, psychological consequences would be a general prevalence of narrow provincial mentality. After bourgeois civilisation, with its tendency of growing cos-

mopolitism and life enrichment, any return to parochical forms of life and thought would constitute a major retrogression.

5) But the decisive question is: does excessive decentralisation *ipso facto* eliminate domination, oppression, exploitation? The answer is no. One huge impersonal Leviathan may be merely replaced by a number of small, personal, local masters. Far from being more beautiful, the small master may be more inconsiderate, arbitrary, frustrated or sadistic. Decentralisation makes sense only when it helps to get rid of master-slave relations. But the crucial question is indeed how to emancipate from masterhood, how to use decentralisation as a means to abolish alienated power both at the level of global society as well as within each community. Only self-governing socialism offers an adequate answer to this question.

# PART II:

## *DEMOCRATIC SOCIALISM*

# 5 Work in Socialism

The term 'work' nowadays covers three entirely different types of activity. For most people both in capitalism and State-socialism it is toil – *alienated labour*: in order to be maximally efficient and productive, in a purely quantitative sense, work is divided into as many simple operations as possible and accelerated by the appropriate technology to the limit of human endurance. In this process the producer cannot employ any of his potential to think, communicate, innovate, beautify. He has no say in the decision-making, no relation to the products of his work. The whole process is meaningless, purely instrumental and rather a loss of life than life itself. Alienated labour disappears in humanistic socialism. What remains is *work* – a socially necessary activity of producing goods and services in amounts sufficient to fulfil basic needs of all members of society. Work is still instrumental and must be distinguished from praxis, free, spontaneous, creative activity which is an end in itself.

Ideally, more and more working activities for an increasing number of individuals approach praxis. In reality a distinction always remains. Work is socially organised, disciplined, inevitably achievement-orientated, regulated by some norms which are obligatory once democratically accepted, involving some division of roles and a minimum of hierarchy that the technological process itself requires. None of this characterises praxis. Nevertheless, the structure and character of work will be profoundly changed in humanistic socialism. Basic changes may be summarised in the following way:

1) Socialisation of the means of work; 2) change of the purpose of work (it will no longer be profit but satisfaction of basic needs of all members of society); 3) self-management; 4) humanisation of the process of work.

## 1 Socialisation of the means of work

Socialisation of the means of work has two meanings which

are compatible with each other, but different from turning private property into State ownership.

In the first sense socialisation of the means of production is the transformation of private property into common social property. That means that land, natural resources, the buildings of factories, machines, means of transport and other equipment would no longer belong to individuals with the right to dispose of them at will, to sell or bequeath them, to appropriate all products. But – and here is the basic contrast to all Statist societies – those means of production will not become the property of the State, where a bureaucratic élite would then achieve the right to dipose of them and to appropriate part of the surplus product in the form of excessively high salaries and material privileges. To be social, common public property means a) to belong to the society as a whole without anybody's right to sell or bequeath it, and b) to be put at the disposal of a working community which would then share the income from the products of work with the rest of society in order to cover both individual and collective social needs. Socialisation in this strong sense is relevant to all those larger enterprises where the process of production has already been socialised but where the appropriation of the income produced has been private. And the justification for socialisation of the means of production is the fact that those means were actually produced by social work, by the accumulated unpaid surplus of work of hired producers over a long period of time.

There is another, weaker sense of socialisation applicable to all those cases where an individual has acquired some property on the means of production by saving from his own past work, without any exploitation of other workers (the small farmer, artisan, or small shopkeeper). He is free to enter into association with other producers (co-operatives, collectively-owned and managed small firms). Such associations would distribute their income (after they pay their share for the satisfaction of general social needs) according to the rules laid down by themselves. They would be free to lay more emphasis on remuneration according to work or on remuneration according to needs. In the former case they might wish to remunerate proportionately to both actual work and past work, objectified in the invested property. Working communities themselves may decide to distribute all income in strictly equal shares. But this cannot be the principle of the whole society. A genuine equity of individuals who have different abilities and needs, and live under different conditions cannot clearly consist in simple equality of income. Some differences in income may compensate the differences in situations and provide really equal opportunities for life.

## 2 Transcendence of commodity production

Once the means of production have been socialised, the whole process of production gains an entirely new meaning. It is no longer production for profit, but for the satisfaction of human needs. This does not rule out any competition or struggle among different particular interests and needs. However, these are conflicts which are not antagonistic, do not involve mutual exclusion, and may be resolved by dialogue and consensus. Since the key to power and domination – property of the means of work – socialised, social conflicts must be regulated and the whole of production and social life cannot but be directed in a democratic way, through negotiation and mutual agreement.

How an economic system which is not based on commodity production might look is very hard to say because we are still far from that level of abundance and general welfare at which a profound change in the motivation of producers can take place and a predominant concern for human needs replace a drive for maximisation of profit which still characterises both advanced forms of capitalism and initial forms of socialism. There are all kinds of problems:

a) What would replace the market economy as the regulative factor? Who is to determine which needs should be satis-, fied and to what extent, and consequently which kinds of commodities (and in what quantities) should be produced? Would not even relatively rational and efficient decision-making on these matters require a huge bureaucratic apparatus and, in practice, a return to a strong, central, political authority which would be able to implement its decisions?

b) Then, how is the economic value of various products and services determined without the market? How are workers remunerated if they no longer receive wages, and the value of the products of their work cannot be clearly established?

c) Is it possible for an economic system to survive and develop without competition on the market? Does not competition encourage all kinds of initiative, ingenuity, and compel present-day enterprises to improve production, invest in scientific research and new technology, open up new possibilities, and create ever new and ever better kinds of goods and services?

d) Is not an economic system in which people are remunerated according to needs basically parasitic and self-destructive? Will not people abuse their new rights? Will they not hoard all kinds of goods which they really do not need, causing unexpected shortages?

e) How can all human needs be satisfied when they change quickly and in many unpredictable directions?

These are formidable problems and we are nowadays hardly at the threshold of an epoch in which conditions might be created for their solution.

Without having an insight into the historical possibilities of their solution all talk about the transcendence of human alienation is mere poetry. The abolition of exploitation is possible in a system of self-government while there is still commodity production. However in such an equitable society in which there is no State and no privileged élite, many forms of alienation might still survive: instead of abolishing the status of the worker as a mere appendage of machinery, all individuals might be compelled to be workers and all their senses might be reduced to one – the sense of having. Consequently overcoming alienation is a much more difficult problem and requires a very advanced level of material and cultural development.

In fact, what allows us to speak about real, historical and not mere logical possibilities of the future is the fact that in the present-day, advanced industrial society there are already some tendencies of the supersession of commodity production in its classical, fully developed capitalist form.

a) Even in capitalism, the market has never been the only regulative factor; and since the rise of twentieth-century monopolies, it is often not even the decisive factor. There is planning within the corporation, there is agreement among corporations, there is intervention of the big banks, there is an increasingly regulative role of the State. In a mixed system of

Statism and self-government the power of directing the process of production is divided between several forces: the market, the State, the Bank (as a social not a privately owned institution), and free associations of enterprises (in a given branch or in a given region, or both). The last two are especially interesting and are basically new forms. A socialist bank does not have any stocks and does not bring any profit to the stockholders. It works with social financial funds – those of the State and of various enterprises, whose representatives decide on basic matters. It invests money not only where it would bring the best profit, but also where the greatest social need is, e.g. for the industrialisation of under-developed regions. Therefore it is partly a non-profit making organisation.

Associations of enterprises are fully an economic form of the future. They supply one another with raw materials and goods, credits, cadres, and information; they aid each other in moments of crisis and join efforts in planning the future. The decision-making within such associations is, or could be, in the hands of the organs of self-government. Within the development of all kinds of free associations of enterprises – not only at the intermediary, regional level but also at the level of global society – it becomes obvious that the functions of co-ordination, regulation and planning can increasingly be performed in a rational and efficient way without State bureaucracy and with a considerably reduced role of the market.

b) Many goods and services have already ceased to be commodities not only in socialism but also in advanced capitalism. The price of basic food stuffs in many countries is not the result of free competition on the market; it is determined by the State, and is sometimes artificially low in socialist countries to keep the standard of living at a reasonable level (and also as an additional form of the taxation squeezed out of the peasants in the process of primitive accumulation of capital). In some countries they are artificially high – much higher than in the world market – in order to create favourable and stable economic conditions for agriculture. Food is sometimes even free, given as an aid to foreign countries, or to the poor within a country.

Drugs are already free in many countries. Gas for heating and cooking is practically free in the Soviet Union (people pay less than one rouble per month) because it is in plentiful supply. Apartments in many countries are not commodities: the rents are considerably below the market price. The same holds for many services: for example, public transport, radio, television, education, health services, social security. Many countries already have free education from kindergarten to PhD courses. There can hardly be any doubt that this tendency will continue both in socialist and in welfare capitalist society.

To the extent to which a system of self-governing socialism develops, a worker ceases to be just a commodity whose labour is exchanged for wages. While his product is sold on the market, it is clear that his income will, on average, be higher than his former wage (because he is less exploited) and lower than the total value of his product (because a part of the surplus product will have to go for the satisfaction of common needs). It seems to me that four criteria must be taken into account in order to determine the value of the work of a worker:

    i) quantity of work, expressed in the number of hours,
    ii) past work, (study, training) needed for acquiring necessary knowledge and skills,
    iii) intensity of work,
    iv) creativity (innovation, improvement).

c) Competition in the market is no longer so important for economic development, even in capitalism. The basic goal of the techno-structure, which is nowadays the carrier of material progress, is *growth* for its own sake: that, in itself, is a criterion of success and brings reputation and prestige.

On the other hand, there is no need to underestimate the importance of economic competition. But it might have different forms from the one which takes place in the market. Best quality in itself – not mediated by the amount of sale – is the indicator of success in competition, and moral recognition gains in importance.

d) The fear that people might abuse their new rights, hoarding more goods than they really need, is the consequence of old habits. People brought up and educated in conditions of scarcity of all kinds tend to behave that way. There cannot be a new wealthy world with old poor people who are still hungry in many respects. However, abundance comes gradually and people get used to it. When socialist health care was introduced in Yugoslavia people used to collect all kinds of drugs and store them. After a few years they realised how stupid and meaningless such behaviour was. The new system was stable and so the reserves of drugs were unnecessary because one was always able to get what one needed and so they had no black-market value.

e) The fact is that 'need' is a historical concept. In some countries or in some past times one 'needed' a bicycle. Some people nowadays 'need' a second, or even a third, car. Priority of needs quickly changes in a developing country. At first most money goes on food, later, at a higher level, on clothing, then interest concentrates on furniture, next is better accommodation, later a car, still later one's own house, travel abroad, expensive hobbies, another car, a weekend house, etc.

It follows then that all human needs can never be satisfied. Even in the most abundant society that one can imagine there will still be a scarcity in some kinds of goods and services.

However, in each historical moment it is possible to determine which is the interval of basic needs in the given conditions, those needs which each individual has the right to satisfy when he works for the society according to his best abilities.

The essential point is, however, that above a certain level of material and cultural development, the most important needs are no longer needs for material goods but a whole range of needs which can be satisfied only through friendship, love, communication and solidarity with other individuals, creative action, and participation in meaningful projects.

The primary interest of a developed man who lives in a materially- and spiritually-rich society is his fellow man, the community; his sense of having becomes increasingly negligible in comparison with all other kinds of new senses and relations in which he expresses all the wealth of his individuality. His most important freedom becomes freedom *to be* and *to become* what he can, not as a result of money and social position, but from his natural capacities.

Once the purpose of production is no longer profit, maximisation of material output loses its present importance. It may be important only in a state of poverty, while material production is not yet sufficiently developed to meet the basic needs of all individuals. Beyond a certain level it loses any sense. Increase of productivity may be used then for a progressive decrease of socially obligatory working hours. This is not so in the present capitalist form of industrial society. During the decade 1967–77 productivity rose 107 per cent in Japan, around 70 per cent in France and Germany and 27 per cent in Great Britain and USA. There was hardly any reduction in working hours and most of the surplus was wasted in over-consumption, armaments and investments into exponential growth, with all its disastrous ecological consequences.

Exponential growth is not necessary in humanistic social-ism. Therefore this seems to be the only form of possible future society that may put a stop to the rapid deterioration of the natural environment. Three problems may be solved at the same time once humankind gets rid of production for selfish particular interests and begins to regulate production ration-ally in order to meet genuine human needs:

a) Present destructive, exploitative relations toward nature would be replaced by a search for more harmony between man and his environment,

b) obligatory work will be reduced and humanised,

c) society will be able to provide more and more facilities for the satisfaction of higher-level communal and psychological needs.

### 3 Workers' self-management and the quality of working life

There are two opposite and unacceptable tendencies in the discussions about the relevance of workers' self-management to the quality of working life. One is to disregard it completely and to look for improvements in the quality of working life within the existing structure of economic and political power. This tendency is characteristic of some Western, social-democratic trade unions which, in addition to the traditional demands for higher wages, also raise issues of social security, further reduction of working hours, limited workers' partici-pation and workers' control. The opposite tendency consists in laying excessive emphasis on the institutional aspect of self-management in its initial, decentralised form, and in believing that the very setting up of a workers' council is able to put a definitive end to oppression and exploitation, to improve human relations and to restore the intrinsic value of work. Many examples of that attitude can be found in apologetic Yugoslav sociological literature that uncritically supports official ideology and glosses over many unsolved problems of the system.

Self-management is indeed a necessary condition of the radical improvement of the quality of working life. The very fact that a workers' council becomes the highest authority in an enterprise implies that some essential changes have taken place:

1) The power of the owners has been abolished, the means of production have been socialised and left at the disposal of workers' collectives. The class of new small owners within the ranks of the workers themselves cannot emerge: stockholding is incompatible with self-management. The only bourgeois institution that may survive in self-managing socialism is buying bonds. But bonds do not give any right to sharing profits – they bring only a limited fixed interest – and, which is especially important, they do not entail any management rights. One man has one vote solely as a worker: his property status is irrelevant.

2) The power of managers and State functionaries is significantly reduced in any genuine self-management. The former are directly subordinated to workers' councils (which can fire them) and are bound by the policy decisions of the council. The latter may pass laws and determine general conditions and frameworks under which all economy will operate, but they have no legal rights to interfere with the decision-making which remains within the jurisdiction of self-managing bodies. Technocracy and political bureaucracy must violate the constitution and the law in order to usurp more power and they will be able to do so to the extent to which socialist consciousness of the workers remains underdeveloped and fails to employ all the new rights and to realise the possibilities that have been offered by new institutional arrangements. This lagging behind of social consciousness is the direct consequence of an insufficiently democratic political life which may have its roots in general material and cultural backwardness, or in specific features of historical development, or in the strong impact of certain external factors.

3) In the absence of all those dominating factors, and to some extent even under least favourable conditions, the

worker in a self-managing organisation gets a chance to become more of a subject in the decision-making process, to reinstate his elementary human dignity, and to create a spirit of genuine collective solidarity. Yugoslav society offers many such impressive examples. Workers at the *21 of May* textile factory in Pirot have turned their factory into a place of beauty, art and culture, a big family in which everybody feels secure and well protected in case of any emergency, but in which no one lives at the expense of his fellow worker. Managers and technicians are paid only workers' wages but the solidarity and cohesiveness of the collective is so strong that they refuse to leave even when they are offered a double salary elsewhere.

Without this emancipatory breakthrough all other changes are limited and superficial.

Human relations in working organisations cannot be improved by education and ideological propaganda alone. An old, but constantly revived, sceptical position says that new men must be educated before a new society is born. An element of truth in this position is that without some highly motivated and deeply committed individuals who are able to live and act up to their moral standards a movement for social change and greater social justice cannot even start. But then, appropriate institutional changes are indispensable in order to produce changes of human relations and behaviour on a mass scale. Thus a relatively small number of middle-class intellectuals created a kibbutz culture with its 'religion of labour' (*dat ha avodah*) and its emphasis on moral value of social and economic equality, on freedom from any formal authority, on group solidarity. However, when a large number of kibbutzim were brought to existence after the Second World War, it became possible to create rapidly a new attitude to manual work, to community and to property in many thousands of young people who joined the kibbutz movement. The fact that the movement has not grown in recent time, in spite of its great achievements, can be explained by the absence of all necessary institutional changes in the broader social context. Small egalitarian socialist islands cannot easily prosper in the ocean of market economy and sharp social stratification.

The experience with Yugoslav self-managing firms is analogous. Not too many people could have been educated in the spirit of self-management while it was only an abstract idea cultivated by small sects of anarchists and libertarian Marxists. When it became a new institutional framework of life for millions of Yugoslav workers, after the conflict with Stalinism in 1948, they quickly began to change their working habits and life-styles. Work became more meaningful, they became much more active, responsible and concerned about maintaining social property and the optimal functioning of the production process. The whole decade following the introduction of workers' self-management in 1950 resulted in spectacular development. Again, the stagnation of the mid-sixties was the consequence of the fact that State bureaucracy imposed an economic policy which favoured market economy, the increase of social differences and the rise of technocracy. All this eventually turned out to be a very unfavourable setting for the further development of workers' democracy and equality.

Another way to underestimate the importance of self-management for the quality of working life is to refer to experiences of 'real socialism' in Eastern Europe. After the victory of a revolutionary socialistic movement there is indeed a period when the initial enthusiasm must be sustained. Rebuilding one's decimated country, the construction of a new, more just society, laying foundations for a better and happier life for one's children are noble ideals which can inspire, make work highly meaningful, and create a true, communal spirit. But when the storms are over and survival assured, a great emptiness follows characteristic of any system in which the State controls all social life and tolerates only what it can control. In the name of economic rationality the State runs the whole economy. It is totally alienated from the workers. There is no way in which workers can influence the operations of this modern Leviathan, even when these operations directly affect their daily work and life, and even when one does not need to be an expert to see that they are far from rational. Work now loses most of its moral value, of its deeper idealistic meaning. The surviving ideals are very abstract – a communist society of equality and brotherhood, without classes and without a State – which is difficult even to imagine in a society in which the social differences and the power of the State constantly grow. No wonder that any remotely idealistic motives are patriotic rather than socialist. What really characterises working life is discipline, maintained by social pressure

and sanction, competitive pride supported by social organisations and mass media, and, above all, the motive of personal
economic improvement. The position of the worker in the
State-owned and State-controlled enterprise does not differ
substantially from that of a worker in capitalist society. He is a
powerless recipient of tasks and orders and reduced to an
appendage of the machine. Technology is the same, organisation of work is the same, hierarchy and subordination to the
foreman and to the manager is the same as in capitalism. His
rights are not the same: more social-economic rights, fewer
political ones. For example, the right to organise and to strike
is no longer admitted – and for the cynical reason that since
workers now constitute the ruling class they need not organise
and strike against themselves.

From this experience an obvious conclusion follows: a mere
replacement of one political centre by another, of one kind of
repressive state by another, of one alienated form of property
by another does not essentially change the social status of the
worker and the quality of his working life.

Self-management is necessary but not a sufficient condition
of the radical improvement of the quality of working life – as
recent Yugoslav experience indicates.

First, the existence of the formal structure of self-
management need not automatically change the character of
human relations in the collective. If workers happen to be (or
are encouraged to be) more interested in issues of distribution
than of production and of communal forms of life, then their
relations may be contaminated with group egoism, conflicting
private and particular concerns, permanent strife and envy.
There will be little solidarity within the enterprise or with
other workers' collectives.

Second, once there is insufficient solidarity in a working
organisation, it is relatively easy for the operative management to develop into dominant technocracy in spite of its
formal dependence on the workers' council. The strength of
the managers lies in their direct access to information, in their
power to take day-to-day technical decisions, and in an ever
open possibility to make a tacit deal with local political centres:
to exchange their political loyalty for the support of powerful
political organisations. The bigger the enterprise, the greater
the opportunities for management to manipulate one group of

workers against another and to co-opt some of the workers' representatives in the workers' council. Workers can effectively counteract technocratic danger only if they overcome group egoism, reach genuine agreement on long-range goals of development, if they, too, keep informed about the state of affairs in the enterprise, if they develop a genuine interest in basic policy issues, and preserve full democratic control over their delegates in the workers' council.

Third, the quality of working life depends essentially on the state of global society. Self-management, even in its initial form, presupposes some emancipatory restructuring of the whole society. However, it may go together with a system which combines moderate State repression with a liberalist market economy, which allows an increase of social differences and widespread corruption. While self-management remains decentralised, disintegrated, reduced only to the level of isolated enterprises, it goes together with a powerful central bureaucracy that appears to protect general social interest, that governs all political life, controls culture and education, prevents a free flow of ideas and social criticism, sets external legal and political limits to self-management and effectively undermines it through its alliance with technocracy.

Fourth, from the fact that workers have legal rights to take policy decisions, even from the fact that in some enterprises they actually use those rights, it does not follow that they will use them in order to humanise work and create a genuine communal solidarity. A new humanistic workers' culture is needed which is different from both narrowly economic culture of traditional trade unionism and from narrowly political culture produced by both liberalist and Leninist Parties.

In order to solve all those problems one need not underestimate the importance of self-management but should generalise it and put it into a broader context of social change. More self-determination is needed at all levels of social organisation – local, regional, national, federal – and not only in the sphere of economy, but also of politics, culture and education.

## 4 Humanisation of work

Once the whole society is restructured in order to create ample room for emancipation, the process of work itself can be substantially humanised. Except in a few advanced countries – notably Norway and Sweden – the problem has been generally neglected. Workers still suffer from extreme boredom in their work and under-utilisation of their abilities, from complete dependence on the machine, from exposure to poisonous materials, noise, dirt and dust, from humiliating control, from utter depersonalisation within huge modern factories. Such problems are not automatically solved by the mere socialisation of the means of work nor even by the introduction of self-management. However, these are essential preconditions for a radical reorganisation of the whole process of work. This radical reorganisation involves the following directions of change:

a) Renunciation of dehumanising technology; choice of alternative technology which allows more individual and group autonomy; more collaboration and communication among workers; more complexity of working operations; more self control.

Sometimes, at least in some branches, this kind of change may be the consequence of the technological process itself – of automation for example. In some industries night shifts could be entirely eliminated using automata which can be programmed and supplied with work for hours without human control. Contrary to expectation work with fully automated machines may turn out to be more interesting than that with semi-automated ones. For example, the work of an operator in a chemical factory is no longer repetitive and does not have any regular, predictable rhythm. It consists of periodical monitoring (which requires great care and responsibility), of long periods of relative inactivity (which can be filled by reading or talking to other workers), and of occasional dealings with crises. The latter as in any problem-solving, requires the full mobilisation of all the intellectual forces of the worker, and considerable ingenuity in order to locate the trouble and repair it as quickly as possible. However, this level of automation is not possible in many branches of material production, let alone services.

An essentially different approach which is always possible is a return to small, even if less productive, enterprises. They offer a better chance of being transparent, democratically run, self-reliant, evenly distributed (avoiding huge pollution concentrations). Above all, they offer a more interesting and a more diverse kind of work. Even from the point of view of present-day economic thinking (the axioms of which will become irrelevant soon) it is clear that modern technology does not exclude smallness. A good deal of recent progress is the transformation of huge, complex instruments and machines into small, simple ones. A future source of energy for a whole country, even for several countries, could be a small nuclear fusion plant. For a country that is only beginning its industrialisation the most rational policy might be to build small enterprises, which would be able to use local raw materials, local labour of limited skills, and inexpensive 'intermediate' technology.

For entirely different reasons the need for small enterprises could emerge in the future in advanced societies. An ecological need to slow down production will coincide with a purely aesthetic need for beautiful, hand-made goods. Highly productive automated plants saturate markets with uniform industrial goods. Elementary needs could be fully satisfied, poverty could disappear entirely. Then the beautiful would slowly begin to prevail over the functional. Craftsmanship would be revived; huge-scale industrial production would lose its present importance because the need for it would begin to decline relatively.

b) Another facet of the humanisation of work is the reorganisation of the process of production. Big systems will be split into smaller units without loss of necessary co-ordination. For example, the assembly-line will be eliminated, productive tasks will be given to relatively autonomous groups of workers, who will divide them among individuals, rotate roles, and determine their own rhythm of production. Control from above will be replaced by self-control and self-regulation.

Another possibility is giving up a too narrow and specialised division of work and designing jobs which are much more complex and interesting, employing considerably more of the workers' mind and imagination. For example instead of repeating the same simple operation time and again, a worker may be responsible for assembling the whole product.

c) This presupposes that the concept of the division of work will undergo a profound change. Division of work will

become increasingly free and flexible, avoiding rigid professionalisation as much as possible. One of the basic tenets in the
new education will be a choice of work according to ability
and other subjective dispositions. This involves free access to
all jobs independently of sex, race, nationality or age. Instead
of being tied to one single role in the process of socially
necessary work during one's whole life, each worker will have
the right to demand a substantial change of his work and to
gain the necessary additional knowledge and skills that would
qualify him for a new role.

d) The physical environment of work could be substantially
improved. The present level of workers' exposure to poisonous substances, to likely accidents, to noise and dust, will in
future be regarded as unbelievably barbaric.

All this holds, however, under the assumption that the
relations of class domination and exploitation would be
abolished in the whole society. Otherwise, 'job enrichment', a
negligible measure of workers' participation, alternative technology, beautification and personalisation of the working
place, serve essentially the purpose of conserving an inhuman,
unjust system by making small concessions and introducing
harmless non-expensive modifications. That explains why
many small reforms are introduced by technocracy in its
efforts to cope with absenteeism, and are sometimes imposed
on workers against their will.

Furthermore there is nothing essentially liberating in a small
enterprise as such. The very fact of smallness does not exclude
the possibility of master-slave relations. Personal, visible masters may be more cruel and oppressive than abstract
institutionalised ones. The road to emancipation and justice is
no more gained by abolishing hundreds of thousands of individual masters than by transforming a couple of abstract master institutions. That is why State capitalism is historically
progressive with respect to early entrepreneurial capitalism.
And that is why the slogan 'small is beautiful' may express not
only a progressive anarchist or socialist idea but also a romantic, retrogressive attitude of dispossesed small landowners,
small businessman or a new strategy of the *status quo* preservation of an enlightened technocratic optimist.

In spite of all these limitations present-day attempts to
humanise work without changing the existing structure of

power have the great merit of exposing a real problem which has been neglected by many movements for social change and workers' liberation.

# 6 Political Power, State, Self-Government

## 1 The concept of power and social justice

All the various descriptions of an unjust society in terms of unequal freedom, of material privileges and special rights enjoyed by certain social élites, of oppression and exploitation of some social groups by other groups, may be generalised as cases of unequal distribution of power. This thesis requires qualification since a general concept of power is ambiguous. At least two distinctions are necessary for our purpose.

On the one hand, the concept involves a distinction between a capacity to dominate and a capacity to create.[1] It is not by chance that these apparently quite different capacities are associated by the same term: 'power'. Both are cases of self-affirmation and self-determination. An individual or collective subject objectifies his thoughts, projects, desires both when he *produces* a new thing, event or situation and when he make other subjects *behave* in the way he wants. Domination and creation may in some sense overlap – as one can witness at a concert of the Berlin Philharmonic Orchestra. Herbert von Karajan in some senses dominates his orchestra and together they create a new interpretation of the work on the programme. However, this is a very sophisticated and exceptional kind of domination: dominated musicians are accomplished creative artists, each one taking an active self-determining part in the musical production, and most experience playing under Karajan as an opportunity for self-development rather than as a process of subjugation and depersonalisation.

In most cases domination and creation are sharply distinguished and mutually exclusive. In creation, the subjective energy that craves for objectification finds its proper outlet in the humanisation of the not yet human, natural things and social institutions. The very concept of creation suggests that the result of the process is something that is not only new, but also a value from the given axiological standpoint. In domination, the goal is shifted from producing a desirable new valuable object to imposing on other human beings a desired pattern of conduct. When it is collective, creation involves a measure of individual autonomy and unique personal imagination. Domination, on the contrary, almost invariably tends to destroy both personal identity, autonomy and imagination, and tends to reduce a person to an object.

One cannot simply say that the power of creation is a natural human capacity whereas the power of domination is merely a social product. Unless a child is socialised in a way that is appropriate to his creative potential, this potential is inevitably wasted; in this sense creativity is social. On the other hand, after several millenia of life in competitive, oppressive societies, a disposition to dominate, especially in a situation where paths to creation are blocked, has become part of man's second nature. In that sense domination is also natural. And yet there are two basic distinctions between the two. A creative disposition is much older, much more deeply rooted – it characterises human life in a most specific way from the beginnings of pre-history. Furthermore, it is a necessary condition of human history: all development, all transcendence of given forms of historical life, are the consequence of the production of ever-new symbols, thoughts, tools, natural environments, social institutions. On the contrary, a disposition to dominate is a very late product of human history and in no sense was it either specifically human or necessary for human survival and historical development.

Another distinction between capacities to create and to dominate is that the former allows democratisation and universalisation, whereas the latter does not. The creativity of one person does not exclude creativity of everybody else – there is an unlimited space for creativity and an unlimited variety of its specific forms. Furthermore, one's ability to produce novelties, to explore new objects, shapes, expressive forms, ideas will only be encouraged and supported in a creative social environment. A creative person will therefore easily subscribe to a demand for creativity in the form of a categorical imperative. Consequently such a demand has an ethical character.

It is quite different with the power to dominate. Domination of the one involves subordination of the other. Self-affirmation of the master involves self-negation of the slave.

Domination of a community by an autocrat or an oligarchy constitutes an essential obstacle to any democratisation. Demand for domination cannot be universalised, it is incompatible with ethics.

Another distinction in the concept of power is very relevant to political theory and to any discussion about the ways to achieve a more just society. This is the distinction between power in the sense of a personal mental ability to influence, to attract, to persuade, to win followers and admirers, and social power, backed by institutions and by actually used or threatened physical force. Both limit or destroy human freedom. The former limits actual choices, the latter reduces the very possibility of choice or, more generally, of self-determination. Necessary conditions of self-determination are:

1) There are at least two real alternatives from which to choose.
2) The given subject S is aware of those alternatives, of their immediate consequences and risk involved.
3) S makes a conscious, autonomous choice.
4) S acts according to his choice.
5) The result of S's action is within the range of expected consequences.

When an individual or group of individuals is only *psychologically* dominated by a strong, attractive, charismatic personality their actual choice is impaired, it becomes heteronomous. Their freedom is then illusory, but objectively the possibility of freedom has been preserved since all other conditions of self-determination are still there. Social domination that rests on coercive force reduces or destroys the very possibility of freedom. The scope of real alternatives that opens up and broadens with increasing self-determination tends now to diminish, or to be reduced to a simple dilemma: choose what social powers expect from you, or else you will be socially degraded, lose your job, end up in jail, perish. Naturally, the dominating social power need not reduce the objective alternatives so drastically, it may efficiently prevent growth of consciousness of all real alternatives, it may so educate or indoctrinate individuals that they are not able to bring to awareness the possibility of different life-styles and of different social arrangements which exist objectively. Or the dominating social power may declare its readiness to tolerate other possibilities but effectively preclude any acting outside certain narrow limits, or it may appear to tolerate legitimate but undesired acts only to intervene in such a way as to render the consequences of those acts totally unexpected and unacceptable to all concerned.

The conclusions of this analysis are the following:

1) A demand for more justice in the sense of a more equal distribution of power does not and cannot possibly mean the levelling of creative power. Diversity of genetic dispositions and of forms of socialisation survive in any conceivable society. Some persons will always be more creative than others. However, there are many different forms of creativity which are hardly comparable. Creative powers are not mutually exclusive, they are rather mutually supportive. Creative power may be democratised and universalised; it is an ethical value. Rather than equal distribution of creative power the purpose of a just society is bringing to life social conditions under which all individuals may maximally realise their specific potential creative powers.

2) In contrast to creative power, the power of domination cannot be universalised, and is ethically bad. A society is just to the extent to which the power to determine actions and to regulate important processes is equally distributed. In other words social justice tends to exclude domination of some individuals and social groups over the others. However, cases of psychological domination will likely survive in any conceivable society. Unless biochemical knowledge is used to determine the characteristics of new-born babies, there will always be exceptionally forceful, brilliant and attractive individuals who will make an impact on their surroundings and tend to assume leadership of groups and communities. Leadership need not exclude autonomous decision-making of those led, but often it does. And yet in so far as leadership is not backed by coercive social institutions, but rests on personal qualities, in so far as it does not reduce or destroy the very possibilities of free choice, it need not be the target of social and political criticism. Differences in social status and esteem will therefore remain in any historically possible form of a just society. A demand for more social justice, for more equal distribution of social power, is the demand to abolish social

conditions which allow differences in status to turn into class differences. In terms of our analysis this is the demand to abolish all those social dominating coercive powers which reduce or destroy the very possibilities of free choice of the members of society.

## 2  Basic dominating social powers

Basic social institutions that make coercive domination possible are:

1) the power of private or State owners of natural resources and technological equipment to take a decisive part in economic decision-making, and to usurp the lion's share of the social surplus product;

2) the power of State bureaucracy to determine basic frameworks of all social activities of common interest;

3) the power of the professional cadres of political parties to mislead the people ideologically, to usurp the mandate given to them by the electorate, to control State machinery, and to rule in an essentially authoritarian way;

4) the power of the ruling élite in hierarchical cultural institutions to impose ideas, values, methods of thinking, norms of conduct, life-styles that support the existing, unjust social order.

1) In all capitalist or State-socialist societies work is a sphere of coercive domination. To the extent to which work is socially indispensable and instrumental to the production of definite goods and services it always involves an element of necessity. Work is organised in a more or less hierarchical way, its operations and rhythm are largely determined by the technology used, its results have to meet certain impersonal norms and standards. It is nevertheless true that work could become increasingly free and creative (could become praxis). There is a choice among alternative technologies, and not all of them are equally dehumanising, do not equally turn the worker into a mindless robot. There is a choice among alternative forms of the organisation of work and not all of them are equally hierarchical and authoritarian. There is a choice between reduction of working hours by quickly increasing productivity of work, and utilisation of growing productivity for an

increasingly consumerist way of life. There is a choice between exponential growth with all its disastrous ecological consequences and a moderate growth with more harmony between man and nature and among men themselves within their communities. These are historically possible choices but they are not actually open in any society which does not own and control its means of production.

Both private and State ownership of the means of production constitute tremendous, alienated, dominating powers. In both cases, as experience amply shows, the maximisation of material output, the greatest possible rentability, the maximal efficiency of work are accepted as basic value principles overriding all other conceivable values such as the humanisation of work, optimal self-development and self-realisation of the workers, increasing autonomy and equality among all participants in the process of production. Such basic criterion of evaluation determines the choice of technology, of the organisation of work, of the policy of growth. Exclusion of other alternatives amounts to destroying the very possibilities of human choice in the process of work.

An individual has no real alternative but to assume a fixed, professional role in a rigid division of work. He is prepared for it during the whole process of education. Neither a private corporation nor a State apparatus is willing to invest into ongoing free training that allows true rotation of work roles. Neither one nor the other is willing to consider any project of humanisation of work unless it at least preserves the given level of rentability, unless it reduces absenteeism or results in some other short-range material benefits.

Another presupposition of freedom is awareness of objectively given alternatives. It does not suffice merely to leave some alternatives open objectively: a certain amount of knowledge and culture is necessary to bring the existence of those alternatives to consciousness, to grasp their full meaning, to be aware of at least some immediate consequences. Neither private corporations nor State-owned and State-controlled enterprises have – for obvious reasons – ever indicated any readiness to improve substantially workers' culture, their understanding of economics and of the general nature of the technological process in which they participate. Neither private capital nor State bureaucracy have any interest in preparing workers for competent, responsible decision-making. Nor are they ready to tolerate any real, significant part of workers in determining basic policies of production. Present-day forms of workers' participation and co-management (*Mitbestimmung*) are important steps toward social justice in comparison with traditional workers' total deprivation of any say in the process of work. But these have until now been only very small steps; the distance passed recently on the road toward a really just self-governing society is still very modest. Where it is larger, it indicates that corporate and State property is on the way to real socialisation.

2) Whatever essential inequalities and injustices emerge in the economic sphere, the State is there to legitimise them and to protect them by force. It is true that the State protects individuals and groups from small and arbitrary injustices and attempts at domination. But it backs large, fundamental, permanent injustices built into the very social system. Behind every lasting form of social domination that overwhelms and crushes the individual there is the State.

In order to avoid any simplification, it should be emphasised that the State performs at least three really important and necessary functions:

a) preservation of a minimum of order and security;

b) mediation among conflicting particular interests of various social groups, regions, nations, races, religions;

c) a proper measure of regulation and co-ordination of basic economic, educational and cultural activities of the whole society.

Any society must have a form of political organisation which successfully performs all those functions. The State happens to be such a form of political organisation that performs those functions in a coercive way, and clearly in the interest of a ruling social group.

The State's direction is invariably undemocratic. Occasional parliamentary elections do not suffice to secure a general direction according to the will of the people.[3] Far from critically examining the basic assumptions of the system, the State essentially extrapolates already existing trends of development. It reacts with repressive measures when people's elementary wisdom and common sense begin to demand changes.[4] In this way the State tends to reduce the basic presuppositions of human self-determination.

The State does not normally operate by opening all existing alternatives, by trying to expand their framework. It feels that on the basis of the general mandate given to it periodically it may be free to decide on all matters of policy, expecting a mere consent by the people. And the whole concept of political education promoted by the State is instrumental to the formation of a loyal, responsible citizen who, out of patriotism, backs his government and who is conditioned to give his consent rather than to think critically about his leaders and their adopted policies.

The State guarantees freedom of thought (which being invisible and uncontrollable hardly needs any guarantee) but not freedom to act accordingly. Civil rights have never been extended in such a way as to include the right of personal integrity in political matters. One is allowed to *think* that a feature of the system is unjust; one is not allowed to undertake *action* to change it. Surely freedom of thought divorced from freedom of action is illusory. By passing laws which make all kinds of reasonable and free activities illegal the State is the most important physical guardian of every unjust society.

3) There are many situations, especially in materially and culturally backward societies, where the only means available to put an end to intolerable injustice is a military *coup* or seizure of power by a revolutionary party. This may be a historically important breakthrough after long stagnation. But neither a professional army nor a Party, led by profressional revolutionary cadres, is able to create a just society.

An army is a part of State machinery – it can only replace one form of the State by another. It can bring about important initial reforms, but its revolutionary potential is limited by the very fact that it acts in an authoritarian way in the name of the people, without really opening the gate to people's self-determination.

A Party may be, but need not be, the part of a political system and of a State. A real social revolution may be led by a political Party. However a real revolution cannot be completed, a new just society cannot be built by a political party. There are certain characteristics of the Party as a form of political organisation that decisively limit its emancipatory capacities.

The primary goal of each Party is to win and keep political power. This is normal in a system of parliamentary democracy with all its advantages over autocratic or oligarchic systems. There are at least several Parties that compete and may win only with some kind of public support. But the essential limitation of that form of democracy is that Parties remain permanent mediators between the people and the State. They usurp the power vaguely delegated to them by the people, identify themselves with whatever they declare to be in the people's interest, and rule over both things and people, promoting themselves into the only historical subject, reducing all other citizens to objects of the historical process.

The social behaviour of a Party reflects its own inner structure. The organisation of each Party is more or less hierarchical and deliberately cultivates differences in status between the leader, his closest collaborators, regional and local leaders, rank and file members, the candidates, the activists, the mere sympathisers. The rest are the 'masses' – a mechanical, inert entity, a mere object to enchant and lead.

Consequently, the decision-making process within each Party is more or less authoritarian: the directives, expression of will, flow in only one direction – from the top to the bottom. Orders must be executed with a satisfactory level of discipline which is heteronomous, involving obligatory rules of social conduct, rather than a matter of internalised, autonomous motivation.

A Party must necessarily have its ideology. It may pretend not to and to be merely pragmatic (as in USA) only when an ideology (in the case of American liberalism) already permeates the whole system and, because it has not been seriously challenged, it ceased to be observable – like the air we breathe. An official ideology invariably rationalises the particular interests of the ruling élite, and justifies the existing social order. It construes the given social form as *the* form of society. It discards important problems and eliminates the very method of critical thinking and of projecting essentially different possibilities of social life. However, a revolutionary ideology (in contrast to a revolutionary theory) equally misleads, although in a completely different sense. It offers a distorted, black-and-white image of reality in which the masses are idealised, the vicious, irrational features of the given system caricatured, the severity of the crises exaggerated, the rival revolutionary forces abused and slandered. In such an ideology the risks and complexities of the revolution are glossed over, or minimised. An early stage of the revolution is construed as *the* revolution. When it is completed, all subsequent development is presented in terms of a mere quantitative growth rather than ongoing social transformation and increasing emancipation. The full realisation of the initial vision of a just society is postponed *ad calendas graecas*.

The purpose of all forms of ideology is to manipulate the masses, to win their passive, unqualified support. An ideologically misled person can no longer be a free, self-determining subject. He is no longer able to see all the real alternatives. To the extent to which he makes any choice it is prescribed by his Party. If he has any doubts he has either to suppress them or to lose his integrity – thinking as a minority and acting in conformity with the majority. Whatever their past merits, political Parties sooner or later become obstacles on the road to more just societies. Political organisations are needed that would perform some of the political functions associated with political Parties but which would be more democratic and less power-oriented.

4) The breeding grounds and promoters of ideologies are not only political Parties but also scientific, cultural and educational institutions, controlled by the ruling élite of unjust societies. Relations in these institutions are invariably asymmetrical and hierarchical. The authority of the academic establishment rests not only on competence and creativity, but also on almost absolute, unchallengeable power to decide on marks, degrees, grants, awards and all similar determinants of both income and status in the world of culture. Such a privileged and powerful cultural establishment will behave as an integral part of the ruling establishment of the whole society. It is only too natural that it will produce values, and impose ideas, norms of conduct, and styles of life that support the existing unjust social order.

## 3  Transcendence of the State

State and self-government are incompatible, but genetically

linked. It is remarkable how often it is overlooked that, on the
one hand, self-government is a principle of political organisation that constitutes a genuine alternative to the State, on the
other hand, 'withering away' of the State (Engels' *Absterben*)
or, more precisely, 'transcendence' (Marx's *Aufhebung*) leads
to a self-governing political structure.

The fact is that there is not much discussion of the 'withering away' of the State in recent Marxist literature. Lenin did
not have time, nor perhaps the will, to put his ideas from *State
and Revolution* (1918) to practice. The last Soviet legal
philosopher to defend the theory of the 'withering away' of
both the State and of law, Evgenii Bronislavevich
Pashukanis,[1] disappeared in 1937. Since then the Soviet State
has concentrated more political and economic power than any
institution in history and does not give the slightest indication
that this growth will be slowed down, let alone reversed.

In Yugoslavia a critique of Statism, of professional politics
and bureaucratism had quite a prominent place in the 1958
Programme of the League of Communists of Yugoslavia. It
was stated clearly that the organs of the State would have to be
transformed into organs of self-government. This process is
still in its initial phase. A relatively decentralised, federal State
still exists alongside a network of self-managing bodies.

Communist parties which may hope to seize power by
parliamentary means in a not too distant future (for example,
in Italy and France) drop the phase of the dictatorship of the
proletariat and discreetly study the possibilities and ways of
the *democratisation* of the State, and of the supersession of a
*bureaucratic* State. This is quite promising as a matter of
immediate practical policy. In contrast to anarchism, even the
most libertarian Marxism will not pass phases of a mere abolition and destruction of the State. Transcendence (*Aufhebung*) is
essentially different from 'abolition' and a transition phase is
needed for it. However, one must not forget Lenin's warning
from *State and Revolution*: the idea of withering away is
directed not only against anarchists but also against opportun-
ists. The phrase 'free people's State', coined by German social
democrats a century ago, made sense only from an agitational
point of view. Scientifically, it was insufficient; strategically it
was opportunist – a 'catch-word devoid of political content', a
'pompous philistine' phrase. Every State is a 'special force' for

class domination. Consequently no State is 'free' and a 'people's State'.[3]

The only long-range revolutionary solution is the transcendence of the State, its structural transformation into a multi-level network of self-governing councils and assemblies. Other alternatives are either liberal or Stalinist. The former was expressed by Kautsky when he opposed 'democratic state' to self-government and said:

It is not quite suitable to speak about State democracy as self-government of the State by the people. People as a whole cannot govern themselves. They need appropriate organs to run things in their organisations. They need them especially in the most powerful among their organisations, in the State.[4]

The latter was inaugurated by Stalin at the 18th Congress of the Bolshevik Party: 'The Soviet State is an entirely new State never seen before in history. While capitalism still exists in the rest of the world it has to stay and increase its power, even in communism.[5]

Nothing reveals better the bureaucratic nature of an opportunist movement nor of a stagnating post-revolutionary establishment than such apologies of the institution of the State.

There are, however, theoretical reasons for a widespread confusion and uncertainty among Marxists concerning the nature and destiny of the State as a political institution inherited from the old class society.

First, the State was defined onesidedly and purely negatively as a mere machine of repression, of class domination. It is more and more obvious that the State has other functions, and that some of these are necessary in any organised society.

Second, the concept of withering away of the State is rather vague and does not offer any criterion as to when precisely an institution loses the character of the State.

Third, the concept of transcendence can be made much clearer. However, any sharp definition involves a decision, and it is always a problem whether that decision will be acceptable to the whole community. It is certainly possible to redefine the term 'State' in such a way that whatever I describe as a transition *from State to self-government* can be reinterpreted as a transition *from bureaucratic to a participatory-democratic State*.

This last question is semantic. The other two are not.

As a matter of fact, the State has at least three other functions in addition to the repressive one (which was so much emphasised by classical Marxist theory):

1) it preserves a minimum of order and security which is an indispensable life-condition for every citizen, regardless of his class;

2) it mediates among conflicting particular interests of various social groups, regions, nations, races, religions;

3) it regulates and co-ordinates the basic economic, educational and cultural activities of the whole society.

1) The State protects both a given social order and indispensable elements of social order in general. The former is clearly repressive. The State has always been and remains an instrument of coercion. In bourgeois society, the State provides the necessary legal justification, but is also ready to use a formidable apparatus of force in order to preserve basic capitalist institutions: private ownership of the means of production, commodity production, free competition on the market, profit as the basic material incentive of the whole economic expansion. In the name of freedom the State blocks any practical engagement for the creation of more democratic institutions. Struggle for participatory democracy is condemned as destructive from the point of view of existing democratic order, characterised by the parliamentary machinery and pluralism of political parties. In present-day Statist-socialist societies a powerful army and security forces protect State ownership of the means of production, administrative planning, the privileged position of the ruling bureaucratic élite, the one-party system. Self-government is resisted by both ideological means – when it is condemned for being a manifestation of 'petty-bourgeois revisionism', as in the case of Yugoslavia – and by force – when units of the Soviet army crushed workers' councils in Budapest in 1956.

Nevertheless, this repressive role must not be confused with the role of keeping an elementary order in the sphere of public life, which must be preserved in each society. Certain inalienable rights and liberties of all citizens (freedom of thought, of conscience, of speech, of organisation, manifestation, demonstration, criticism of public officials) must be protected; they may be enlarged but not jeopardised. Individuals must be protected against the criminal and pathological activities of other individuals. Independence and security of the nation or of federation of nations must be defended against possible outside aggressors. These roles do not necessarily require a professional army and police force, they could be better performed by more effective and less dangerous institutions of self-defence. In recent times the army and the police have acted far more frequently against their own people than against foreign enemies.

2) In every society some kind of central agency is needed to mediate and arbitrate among various particular interests. No matter how high a degree of unity among different social groups (classes, nations, races) there is also a certain degree of pluralism, or mutual struggle. The State apparently defines a general interest and lays down a general framework of legal norms for the resolution of conflicts. It pretends to be impartial, but it is not. While self-government is the real manifestation of the general will of the people, the State is ultimately an expression of the particular will of the ruling bureaucracy. Once the State creates an élite of professional politicians, this élite will inevitably constitute a particular interest of its own, but will use all available ideological means to hide it and rationalise it.

3) With growing complexities of modern society and increasing risks involved in big production and its highly efficient technology, the State plays an ever greater *regulative* role. It interferes more and more in order to preserve certain necessary proportions, and especially a sufficient growth of energy supply, to discourage certain economic trends and support others, to protect the citizen from an intolerable level of abuse by big corporate powers, to control productive forces that can be used for large-scale, violent purposes, to preserve or restore a reasonably healthy natural environment, to secure a satisfactory level of education and other public services, to take care of social welfare, and to support scientific and cultural development.

These functions are indeed necessary and to deny this would be both unrealistic and retrogressive. We cannot go back to *laissez-faire* arrangements of a technologically primitive and small-scale ecomomy, and of a population with an inferior political culture.

However the concept of *transcendence of the State* involves a significant amount of preservation of such functions; the particular class interest that was served by regulation and mediation will be replaced by a general need to maintain and improve an already reached level of human civilisation. On the other hand, the concept of transcendence of the State involves the abolition of the essential limitation of every State: its repressive function. A new, really liberating and more just social order, will naturally be supported by the majority of population. Once it wins their support for its programme and manages to prevail against the force of an oppressive establishment, it will be able to hold on against that same defeated establishment if it really begins to bring its programme to life. Justice for all, democratically accepted general norms and sanctions holding for all citizens, must be sufficient to defend the achievements of revolution. There can be no justification for applying special repressive measures, for using indiscriminate 'red terror', against any individuals or groups, because they merely belong to a certain class and advocate the ideology of that class. From this point of view the term 'dictatorship of the proletariat' is indeed misleading. It either means ' proletarian democracy' – the rule of the majority of people – in the sense in which it was actually used by Marx. Or it makes room for unnecessary and unjustifiable arbitrary violence of a ruling oligarchy, which was the interpretation of Stalin and Stalinists.

Transcendence of the State is certainly not an instant act – it is a historical process in which two kinds of change take place. On the one hand, new institutions of public power emerge alongside the State and assume more and more roles which traditionally belonged to the State. On the other hand, the quality of these new public institutions is essentially different from that of the State: they are organs of *self-government*.

Everywhere in the modern, developed world there is a strong tendency for the State to assume too many roles, very much beyond what is reasonable and necessary. The hypertrophy of the State in some quasi-socialist countries is a drastic case: the State does not only fully control political life, material production and exchange, but also all education and culture – indeed all spheres of social life. This tendency must be and can be reversed: it generates a totally bureaucratic society and there is a widespread sense of danger. However, because a mode of dualistic thinking is deeply rooted in Western culture, most people continue to think in terms of dichotomies: either the State or a regression to privatisation; either centralism or an ineffective decentralisation; either competent bureaucrats or incompetent laymen in charge of important social affairs. But there is a third, self-governing solution.

There may be institutions which are neither State nor privately controlled, which cannot be a source of alienated power either of professional bureaucrats or of wealthy individuals. They need not be organised and run either in a thoroughly centralistic nor in a loose, decentralised way. The rule should be that as much regulation and mediation as possible (depending on the nature of the problem) should take place at lower levels of social organisation – in enterprises and local communities, in particular regions and branches of activity. Only when the problem, the conflict, the danger, transcends the limits of a given community, should it be placed in the hands of the next higher self-governing authority, where it will be solvable. In other words, a tendency of decentralised decision-making (concerning particular social needs) does not exclude a necessary minimum of centralised democratic regulation (concerning the needs of the whole society).

The real dilemma is not between competent professionals or non-competent laymen. Professionals invariably have one limited kind of skill which is in addition limited to one special field. They have technical skill (know-how) for a narrow area of problems but not, as a rule, a deeper, wide-range, theoretical understanding (know-that), nor life experience, and a clear value-orientation concerning the basic choices to be made (know-what). They may be indispensable for selection of the most adequate means when the ends have been already defined. But they are poorly prepared for the choice of ends, of long-range projects for the determination of policies. This kind of task requires a different sort of competence to be found in persons of wisdom and integrity across the lines of professional division of labour. The real dilemma is therefore whether professional experts will be employed for precisely those roles for which they are really competent, fully responsible to the elected representatives of the people, or whether the strings of power politics will be pulled behind the ideological screen of 'professional competence' and expertise by unknown 'grey eminences'.

During the period of rapid development of self-government in Yugoslavia during the fifties and the sixties it was quite visible how an increasing number of State functions were transferred to the organs of self-government: management of State enterprises, of banks, of foreign trade, local authorities, regulation of every-day life, regional co-operation, transport, the health service, education, social security and welfare, mass culture, scientific culture, and partly also defence.

Another essential feature of the process of transition from the State to self-government is the change of quality of public institutions. Theoretically speaking, this is the process of abolition of alienated political power and the professional political structure which disposed of it. The practical meaning of this transformation may be summed up in the following way:

a) The members of a self-governing body, at any level of social organisation, are directly elected by the people or delegated by a lower-level organ of self-government. The procedure of election is fully democratic: no candidate can have any privileges because of his professional role, past merits or backing by existing political organisations.

b) The members of the self-governing body are elected for limited periods; the principle of rotation must be strictly observed and excludes perpetuation of power of professional politicians.

c) The members of self-government are directly responsible to their electorate (and not to any political organisation). They are obliged to give account regularly to the community which they represent and are subject to recall. Such dependence on the will of the community does not preclude their leadership role. They lead by articulating and stating explicitly the vaguely felt needs of the community, but also by finding ways to reconcile particular interests of the community with interests of other communities and of society as a whole. The institution of self-government excludes authoritarian leadership: the will of the people must count at all times, and the use of force is out of the question. But it does not follow that the roles are simply reversed and that the elected representatives have no other alternative but to follow blindly every twist and turn of the mass current. In case of conflict they will make an effort to prevail by the strength of their arguments – or else they will resign. The road to becoming a career politician is closed anyway. And the community is strongly motivated to have able representatives.

d) Representatives must not enjoy any material privileges. They may be compensated for their work as in the case of any other creative public activity. Anything beyond that level constitutes a concealed form of exploitation, produces undesirable social differences, lowers the motivation of the representatives as well as the morale of the community, and eventually leads to the creation of a new, alienated social élite.

e) An organ of self-government constitutes the supreme authority at the given level. That is where it differs from analogous organs of participation, co-management or workers' control which have only advisory, consultative or controlling functions and, at best, only share authority with political bureaucracy, capitalists or techno-structure. 'Self-governing' institutions presuppose elimination of all ruling classes and élites; professional, technical management must be subordinated to them. They create basic policy, formulate long-range goals, establish rules, decide about cadre issues, control the implementation of accepted policies.

f) While there might be a plurality of organisations that mediate between people and self-governing institutions, none of them must be allowed to assert itself as a 'tutor' over self-government. They could play useful and indeed necessary social roles: to express specific group interests, to educate people politically, to mobilise them for alternative programmes of development, to contribute to the creation of powerful public opinion. But none of them, neither a political Party, nor a trade union, church, nor any other pressure group must have a control over the institution of self-government. Whatever the personal affiliations of an individual elected representative, his loyalty must go directly and fully to the people whom he represents, and not to any mediating organisation.

g) All power of self-governing bodies is delegated to it by the people from the given field and not allocated from the centre. When social power is alienated, all decision-making goes from the top to the base of the social pyramid. When it is not, it is always the lower level of social organisation, closer to the base, which decides how much regulation, co-ordination and control is needed at the next higher level. According to such decisions a certain amount of power is, then, delegated to it. In such a way the authority of the central federal assembly rests on that of national or regional assemblies, and all of them are ultimately authorised to decide on certain issues by the councils of basic working organisations and local communities. Learning from experience in a quickly changing world will give rise to changes of the whole structure: with a growing sense of ethnic identity, mass culture will be increasingly decentralised; on the other hand, scarcity of energy requires the joint effort of the whole society, and a considerably higher level of co-ordination and overall control.

Clearly, the problem is not only one of central decision-making but also the source of authority for it. In a bureaucratic, repressive State, classical liberal doctrines of 'social contract', sovereignty of the people and 'majority rule' serve to legitimate a situation in which all power stems from a relatively small oligarchy, even when it is considerably diffused and decentralised. In self-government all power originates from the councils in the atomic social community, even when a considerable amount of it has been delegated to higher-level self-governing institutions.

## 4  Law in participatory democracy

The new concept of democracy based on the principle of equal self-determination and its corollary, self-government, surpasses existing forms of democracy in two essential respects: a) it embraces not only the *political* sphere but also the whole sphere of *public* life. The concept of democracy is generalised in such a way as to extend also to all those economic and cultural issues which are of such general importance that they require public regulation; b) it involves a shift from *representative* to *participatory* democracy.

This kind of democracy is possible in a society in which all centres of alienated political and economic power have been abolished, and in which the traditional democratic principle of the sovereignty of the people has been fully realised. This need not be a fully egalitarian society: the right to equal self-determination, applied to different undividuals with vastly

different talents and aspirations, will certainly produce a plurality of ways of life, and considerable individual differences in
material wealth, tastes, skills, achievements and social esteem.
But it will preclude emergence of class domination. Power to
accept basic policies, to control their implementation, to distribute products of work remains in the hands of self-
managing councils and assemblies. Law is still needed as an
instrument for minimum social order and conflict resolution
but it is no longer a means of class rule.

In comparison with the legal system in liberal capitalism,
law in socialist participatory democracy differs favourably in
the following respects:

1) Power that passes legislative acts in a parliamentary
democracy is still considerably alienated. It is true the members of a parliament have been democratically elected, but
election has been considerably determined by the general
strength of the élitist political Parties, by the level of electoral
expenditure, by the support of business-governed mass
media, and sometimes also by the aid of existing State and
military machinery. In a system of participatory democracy,
Parties do not rule and do not compete for power, private
capital does not exist, mass media are socialised, and bureauc-
racies dismantled. Laws will be passed by delegates who are
much more – and more directly – responsible to their electorate. This is not incompatible with leadership, and cannot
wipe out any distance between the general will of the people
and the will expressed in the law. However this distance will
be considerably reduced.

2) In any society governed by a ruling class there will be a
strong emphasis on tradition, and the older the ruling class the
greater the lack of balance in the law between tradition and
necessary innovation. Constitutions and some Statutes in
Western democracies are centuries old. This provides some
kind of stability, but blocks social change. From the point of
view of equal self-determination each social group, each new
generation, and indeed each individual, has the right to challenge the reasonableness and justice of the constitution and of
any legal constraint under which he is supposed willingly to
live. Law must be open, revisable and subject to ongoing
popular critical appraisal. This need not jeopardise all tradition: each society needs its accumulated past experience, and

tends to preserve a good deal of its identity. However a living and developing society also needs constant re-interpretation of its traditions and restructuring of its legal framework. Social forces that tend to block radical change will be seriously weakened in participatory democracy.

3) Political and legal decisions are customarily made by a majority vote in a parliamentary democracy. In a uniform society that remains a simple and efficient democratic procedure. In a stratified society, where opposite groups differ in size, the majority vote may become a means of repression against the minorities. That is why a superior method of decision-making in all complex and sensitive issues must be dialogue, negotiation and voluntary consensus. In that sense any rule over the people must indeed be terminated.

4) Of course this does not solve the problem of possible irrational, destructive, pathological behaviour of some individuals and groups. With all respect for pluralism and dissent, certain things must not be allowed in any society, and one of them is tyranny of the weak, and blackmail of the vast majority by the egoistic minority. A law is no longer a law if it is not binding and if it cannot be enforced. There are good reasons to believe that an increasing amount of social issues which are now legislated will be more and more regulated by moral norms and other non-binding and non-enforceable rules. While law still exists it is backed by some kind of tangible force. In parliamentary democracy the apparatus of force is the professional army, the police, security intelligence, and a network of prisons. This force is alienated from the people, and their main purpose is to prevent any radical social change. A participatory democracy is open to change and makes room for each particular interest which may be reconciled with established general interests (stated in the constitution and obligatory while the constitution is still valid). An activity becomes socially pathological when it pursues, beyond any tolerable limit, certain particular interests which are not and cannot be legitimated. Organs of social self-defence which try to stop such egoistic and aggressive activities are not there to punish, to take revenge or to destroy but merely to prevent damage, to block the aggressor – leaving self-governing organs to resolve conflicts. It is of essential importance that decision-making power in organs of social self-defence is not

in the hands of professionals, but belongs to elected and strictly-controlled public servants.

This whole emancipatory trend of legal change is not only contingent upon dismantling present-day monopolies of power and the establishment of a new participatory democracy, but also upon the emergence of a new culture. The basic cultural change consists in a shift from an egoistic power to dominate towards a power to create. This involves a radical re-orientation of all education. Preparation for specialised roles in the social division of labour will lose its present-day importance, and will increasingly be treated as a matter of secondary importance, which it is. The primary goal of all education becomes self-understanding, discovery of one's creative potential, and preparation of an adequate, basic life-project.

This model of a new, participatory democracy and a more just law is not a mere derivative of philosophical thought, it also expresses some real trends and aspirations in the present-day, historical epoch. It is no more utopian than Locke's model of representative democracy was in eighteenth-century England, and Hegel's model of constitutional monarchy was in nineteenth-century Germany. It is by no means a picture of a perfect society: new riddles and conflicts will emerge which we cannot yet anticipate because they are beyond the horizon of our epoch. And yet, from the point of view of emancipatory praxis, a legal system of this type seems to constitute the most interesting alternative to both decaying liberalism and aggressive bureaucratism.

## Notes

1 Pashukanis, *The German Theory of Law and Marxism*, Moscow 1927. In a later work ('The Soviet State and the Revolution in Law', *Sovetskoye gosudarstvo i Revolutiya Prava*, No. 11–12 (1930), pp. 17–49, 237–80) he conceded the possibility of State power becoming stronger in socialism. It did not help him.
2 Lenin, *The State and Revolution*, ch. I, section 4 (in *The Lenin Anthology* by R.C. Tucker, New York: W.W. Norton & Co. 1975 pp. 321–3.
3 *Ibid*, p. 323.
4 Karl Kautsky, *Die materialistische Geschichtsauffassung*, Berlin, 1927, Bk II, p. 461.
5 Stalin, 'Report to the 18th Congress of the CPSU (b),' in *Problems of Leninism* (Moscow, 1945), pp. 632–8.

# 7 The New Legal Institutions for New Social Relationships

The historical possibility of new legal institutions is one of the most neglected issues in contemporary social theory. The analysis of legal institutions in various present-day societies is usually structuralist and functional. It is static and abstracts institutions from social relationships which are embodied and reinforced by them. Most of the future research that has flourished in Western Europe and USA during the last decade hardly deals at all with the necessary transformation of social relationships and corresponding legal institutions. This lacuna can be accounted for methodologically and politically. The customary methods of statistical extrapolation and model building, which give interesting results when applied to the study of new technologies, of demographic changes, of pollution, depletion and other ecological issues, turn out to be too simple and inappropriate to the exploration of new forms of social organisation. But imaginative projections expressing ethical needs rather than describing real possibilities sound too romantic and utopian. It seems, then, that a too narrow, basically conformist, scientific empiricism and a too broad, scholarly disreputable, romantic utopianism are the only two alternatives from which to choose. But there is a third possibility: the method of transcendence, characteristic of critical social science. It makes room for both quantitative and qualitative analysis, realistic description and bold construction, the structural and the historical, the factual and the ethical. All these are necessary elements of any method of inquiry that tries to establish optimal human possibilities at a given historical situation. The reason why this method is not being developed and applied by scholars committed to the preservation of social *status quo* is quite obvious: it is subversive, it introduces a boldness of research that no establishment can fully tolerate.

It is less obvious, however, why there are so few interesting insights into the institutions of the new society in the writings of radical scholars. In order to understand why, for example, Marxist literature is so scanty on this issue one has to take into account, first, the attitude of Marx himself, then the failure of 'the first socialist country' to produce and maintain really new institutions, and finally the biased character of theoretical reaction to this failure.

Marx influenced even the best and most original of his followers by his strong reluctance to make any concrete, long-range, positive predictions or prescriptions. This was partly a wise attitude, since nothing is so perishable in a theory as forecasts of this type. However, his attitude was very much determined by the current conceptions of scientific method. In opposition to utopian socialism, Marx made enormous efforts to render his theory as scientific as possible. It is true that his conception of science, in contrast to the positivism of his time, involved a great emphasis on critique and fortunately, he was not able altogether to refrain from expressing any of his visions of the future. And yet no one fully escapes the limitations of his epoch. Nineteenth-century science was deterministic, and even such an activistic thinker as Marx could not help talking about revolution as a 'necessary' consequence of certain 'iron laws' of social development. But it makes a great difference whether one believes that a new society is *necessary* or is only *possible*. In the former case the concrete forms of the new society are an issue of secondary importance: they will be generated in social practice anyway. In the latter case one must know in advance and as concretely as possible how the possibility looks to the realisation of which he chooses to commit himself.

There was an additional reason why, speaking about the State, the law and the politics in future society, Marx was particularly restrained, and remained satisfied with sweeping generalisations about the transcendence of all these typical 'spheres of alienation' and about the 'dictatorship of the proletariat' as the form of the State in the transition period. Because of his over-optimistic view of human nature and of the proletariat Marx overlooked the danger (intuited already by Rousseau) of the alienation of the *avant-garde* from its own class. In what way, under what conditions, and indeed whether this danger can be avoided at all and the true workers' State realised constitute the most formidable problem of the whole 'transition period'. Awareness of the problem would have surely necessitated a more concrete account of the legal and political structure of the new society.

That the way Stalin interpreted and implemented the 'dictatorship of the proletariat' was a far cry from Marx's original insight there can be little doubt. Soviets were genuinely new institutions. But they lost any substance surprisingly quickly and the social realities that emerged were in blatant contradiction with expectation. Overwhelming bureaucracy firmly in possession of all economic and political power, State property, massive State organs of security and defence, authoritarian planning, were hardly the appropriate institutions for the expected new social relationships of equality and solidarity.

At this point the crucial issue of the State in socialism had to be taken up and clarified. The theory had either to adjust to whatever in reality passed under the name of socialism, or it had to condemn reality in the name of basic socialist aspirations. That is where Marxists divided. Some continued to preach old dogmas, blind and aloof, as if nothing had happened during a whole century; some transformed Marxism into an apology of a bureaucratic State-collectivism; some developed it as a critical theory that sought to transcend, at least in thought, both neo-capitalist and post-capitalist forms of contemporary society. The problem does not exist for the first group, and it is obviously subversive for the second. The interesting question is why it was neglected by the third. This deplorable neglect is probably due to certain deficient interpretations of the basic Marxist ideas of humanism and of dialectic.

Humanism is often construed as a purely philosophical, and therefore an abstract concern about man and the human condition. The basic weakness of this humanism is a lack of almost any mediation between an alienated contemporary world and a possible future world in which man lives in a genuine community and becomes a being of praxis. From this point of view, legal and political institutions, precisely because they are institutions, lead to narrow specialisation, fragmentation and reification of man. The free, creative life of humanity in future need not be unorganised, anarchical, but the organisation no longer has the form of 'institutions', it is much more flexible, spontaneous, much less subject to stable forms and rules. Granting all this, one can still wonder how the transition from one world to the other is at all possible. What then is the missing link between reifying political institutions and non-institutionalised social decision-making? How is the jump made from the classical State to the federation of workers' councils; from the standing army to the armed people; from the police to citizens' self-control; from rigid bureaucratic planning to a non-compulsory, self-determining co-ordination of production; from authoritarian schools to some entirely new forms of education that would not lose any organised systematic character in order to gain in freedom and creativity?

This humanism without mediation goes together with a dialectic that construes transcendence as a merely negative challenge, as a rejection, even a destruction, of the old form. It is by all means essential for transcendence (*Aufhebung*) that it involves the abolition of those defining characteristics of a system that limit and impede its further development. Such inner limitations of the legal institutions in a liberal capitalist society are, for example a very low level of citizen participation in social decision making; favouritism of the State with respect to the wealthy classes; lack of co-ordination and rational direction in most spheres of social life, a tremendous amount of built-in competition and violence. Some of these were partially overcome in societies where successful socialist revolutions took place, but some took quite drastic forms, for example a concentration of immense political and economic power in the hands of political bureaucracy. Without the removal of such structural impediments considerable historical possibilities for further development would be wasted. However the creation of a new social form, characterised by a higher degree of freedom and equality, presupposes the incorporation of many present- and past-institutions of universal and lasting value. That legislative, executive and judicial powers must be separated, that local communities should be relatively autonomous with respect to central government, that political leaders need not be professionals for life but elected for limited intervals, that mass media should be independent of the government, that workers should participate in running their enterprises, that human individuals must have certain rights irrespective of the nation, class, race, religion, sex and generation to which they belong, these are instances of certain rules and institutional patterns that have been achieved after centuries of human struggle, and which are indispensable to a more egalitarian and just future society.

These introductory methodological remarks lead, then, to the following conclusions:

1 Legal institutions are not merely an expression of certain basic social relations; they are also objective constitutive factors of those relationships, especially in a dramatic epoch of revolutionary social change.

2 The experience of twentieth-century social revolutions indicates that the question of the political structure of the new society must be central to debate and solved *before* the revolution rather than left to the discretion of the leaders. One need not have any illusion that the practical creation of a political structure will simply be the implementation of an *a priori* project. It will be contingent on the distribution of political power within the victorious revolutionary movement. However, the fact is that a clear and concrete *a priori* conception of a democratic political structure would considerably strengthen anti-bureaucratic forces.

3 A conception of radically new legal institutions need not be construed as a blueprint for a perfect society. The value of such a conception is necessarily relative to the essential needs and the spiritual horizon of the given historical epoch, although, as we have seen, it could carry in itself elements of universal lasting value. Instead of simply postulating, in a utopian way, what new institutions there ought to be, it would be methodologically more sound to show how a number of problems could be solved by transcending the existing institutions.

The crucial problems of building up new legal institutions for a more free and just society are:

1) How to transcend the government by self-government?
2) The central organs of self-government in a complex modern society could dispose of considerable powers. How does one separate those powers in order to prevent their possible alienation and eventual concentration in the hands of an oligarchy or of a popular dictator?
3) How is a necessary measure of co-ordination and rational direction secured, without destroying the benefits of a relative decentralisation?

4) How is personal security achieved, and the capacity to defend the society from outside dangers assured without resorting to traditional oppressive organs, such as the police and the army?
5) What kind of political organisations are compatible with a true participatory democracy?
6) What institutions are necessary to secure equal conditions for the development of minorities, especially those national, racial and sex groups who have been underprivileged in the past?
7) Which new institutions are needed to protect the human rights of the individual (and not only as a citizen but also as a producer and a consumer) from the wrong-doings of the social institutions themselves?

## 1 Institutions of self-government

If freedom of human individuals is not to be reduced to a few civil liberties but is to be implemented as self-determination in all aspects of social life, if social equality is not to be reduced to equality before the law and equality of opportunity but is to be realised as equality of condition, then the whole structure of power must be changed radically.

Competent administrators, technical experts and managers are needed in the new society, but will have to lose their present power of ruling over people and will have to be fully subordinated to the organs of self-government. The institution of self-government embraces a huge network of councils and assemblies constituted at different levels of social reality and on both territorial and productive principles. One would have to distinguish clearly among at least four levels:

– Basic organs of self-government in most elementary working and living communities.

– Organs of self-government in larger associations, enterprises, communes.

– Organs of self-government for the whole branches and regions.

– Central organs of self-government for the global society.

The basic level of self-government is characterised by *direct democracy*. It is essential that each individual gets the right (although not a duty) to participate directly in decision-making in the most elementary units of social life – both in the assemblies of small enterprises or departments of larger enterprises, and in the assemblies of all inhabitants of a small residential area. Each individual would thus have a chance to express and affirm himself not only as a citizen, but also as a producer and consumer. In Yugoslavia, in small enterprises of less than thirty workers, all are members of the workers' council (in larger enterprises they elect representatives). It should, however, be a matter of principle that each individual producer has an opportunity to act as a subject within the social process of production at least at the most elementary level instead of transferring all his rights to his representative. Another important direction for further development of the Yugoslav model is the creation of territorial organs of direct democracy in which, among other things, each citizen would have an opportunity of defending and promoting his interests as a 'consumer'. (The term consumer should be taken here in the widest sense, that is, not only as a consumer of material goods, but also as a being who takes pleasure in cultural goods, enjoys natural surroundings, creates new social conditions for an increasingly rich and articulate use of free time.)

Basic organs of self-government must have the right to decide how much power they want to transfer to higher-level organs, or, in other words which co-ordinating and controlling functions they wish to delegate to their representatives at higher levels of social organisation.

The next level is constituted by councils of larger working associations and the assemblies of larger and more complex local communities (communes). Most modern industrial, agro-industrial, commercial and other enterprises are so big, and embrace so many different kinds of work and services, that occasional referendums and assemblies of all workers remain the only feasible forms of direct democracy. Councils composed of the elected representatives of all employees practically become the highest authority in the enterprise. They lay down basic policies, plan the production, nominate and supervise the managers, decide about working conditions, distribution of income, harmonisation of interests with other enterprises, contributions for the needs of the local community and the whole society. Councils in the schools, hospitals, cultural institutions have corresponding functions. Assemblies of the communes, are responsible for the whole policy of development of a relatively self-sufficient, territorial community, the optimal size of which is of the order of magnitude of several dozens of thousands of inhabitants. A certain fraction of the surplus work of all producers from the territory of the commune goes into communal funds and is used for financing education, culture public transport, social security, health services, housing, recreational facilities, and, to some extent, investment into new productive capacities. Workers' councils and communal assemblies are limited in their decision-making by the existing legislation and accepted policies of the higher level organs of self-government, but in a true system of self-government the laws are not imposed from an authoritarian centre but, on the contrary, the centre has been delegated power to pass them, and therefore they can be revoked if they stop serving any useful social purpose.

Another higher-level intermediary level is constituted, by the co-ordinating self-governing boards for the whole branches of activity (energy production, metal industry, agriculture, transportation etc.), and by the regional organs of self-government co-ordinating the development of all communes from a definite area. Once bourgeoisie and regional or national bureaucracy have left the historical stage, the purpose of better organisation, co-ordination and direction is no longer increasing efficiency in the struggle against other nations or regions, or in controlling the market. The main purposes of co-ordination are now the elimination of waste, reduction of friction, joining forces for the solution of ecological problems, mutual aid and solidarity, especially aid for accelerated growth of the weak and underdeveloped. Some Yugoslav branch associations offer a good example of increased rationality within a bigger system, although one would have to take into account that the Yugoslav economy at present is both too competitive and exposed to compulsory, authoritarian measures of the regional and central political bureaucracy – thus an important element of solidarity and full autonomy is still missing. Interesting new intermediary forms of self-government were Yugoslav communities for science, education and culture in the late sixties, (before they underwent considerable bureaucratisation). They were not part of the

State apparatus and were run by the elected representatives of corresponding scientific, educational or cultural institutions. Financing these communities was independent of the State budget and State administration; it was regulated by special laws that allocated a fixed percentage of national income for the needs of education, science and culture.

Self-government at the level of global society does not yet exist in any country in its systematic, integral form, although some of its elements have existed in political theory and political practice in various liberal countries.

If there was anything rational in the social contract theory it was the idea that political power must rest on the assumption of the people's voluntary surrender of a part of their natural liberty in order to gain security within a political society. But the idea need not go together with Hugo Grotius' or Hobbes' justification of the absolute monarchy, where the assumption is that in the social contract the citizen surrenders *all* his rights and for *ever* – even the right of resistance to the sovereign when he reigns for his own good. It is also independent of Locke's liberalist justification of the permanent existence of the State, where the contract is located in the distant past and is irrevocable in order to preserve private property. When one gets rid of all obsolete, unhistorical and apologetic elements of the social contract theory, what remains, as the sound core, is the idea of *popular sovereignty*. The original and ultimate power lies in the people. One should remember Jefferson's idea that the dead must not rule over the living and that, therefore, each new generation has the right to rebel against the laws passed by the preceding generation (an idea forgotten both in capitalism and socialism). Popular sovereignty will then mean precisely this: members of a community have the fundamental right (underlying all legal structure) to challenge, re-examine and transcend any existing rule, law, institution or constitutional clause. Consequently, they have the right to decide how much order and what kind of order they wish to have, which social activities and social functions should be supervised, planned and co-ordinated and to what degree of power. Thus they might decide that all supervision of what people think and believe must stop, whereas public control of both quantity and quality of production must be increased. Or they might decide that organs of self-government should be given little power in matters of culture, more in matters of production planning, and quite a lot of power to prevent obvious waste, deterioration of life conditions, or violation of human rights. Decisions of this type will be taken by referendum, or in some other suitable democratic way, after extensive discussion in free mass media. The more accumulated historical experience, is available to a community through persons of knowledge and culture, the more reasonable these very basic decisions will be. Surely some of the historical wisdom is already present in given institutions, and no community would ever wish to destroy all tradition and start *ab ovo*. On the other hand, there is every reason to assume that a community will learn from experience much quicker once there are no powerful interest groups to impede the learning process and preserve the *status quo*.

All other defining characteristics of self-government are also present in various systems in incompletely developed forms. The bourgeois revolution has already contributed the idea that administration, the government, the military must be subordinated to the people's representatives, and to parliament, and that the representatives must be democratically elected for limited terms of office, responsible to the people, always subject to recall, and relatively modestly rewarded for their work. There is vast and conclusive evidence from the last two centuries for a very basic principle of self-government, namely that being an excellent leader does not require professional expertise. Some of the best presidents, congressmen, senators, members of parliament and of government have not been professional politicians, and some have not even been intellectuals. The novelty of self-government is, however, removal of all pressures and influences emanating from power accumulated and concentrated in the past, as a result of either traditional privileges, or wealth or past merits. The candidacy or election of a representative will no longer depend on funds available to run the campaign, on acceptability to the Party bosses, to the army or to the Church. A 'democracy' approaches self-government only to the extent to which the outcome of elections would primarily and effectively depend on the personal qualities of the candidates, on their individual competence, integrity and identification with the real needs of the people, rather than on all kinds of ghost-like qualities that money, propaganda and big backing organisations can lend to a rather insignificant and unreliable character.

The central organ of self-government, federal assembly or congress of people's representatives, must integrate both networks of self-governing institutions, one covering various types of activity, the other various territorial communities. There are many possible forms of its inner organisation but all have to take into account the following three necessities:

The first is reconciling the particular interests of various types of activity with the particular interests of various regions.

The second is to reconcile particular interests of various professional and regional groups with the common interest of the whole society.

The third is to preserve the unity of authority in order to secure efficiency and to reduce wasteful inner conflicts, but at the same time to separate power in order to prevent a dangerous concentration of power in the hands of an oligarchy or a single dictator.

1) As to the first, two chambers are obviously needed. One would be constituted of the representatives of all workers (i.e. all who live on the income from their work; in a society without capital workers are all employees in material production, services, intellectual work, administration). The second chamber would be constituted by the representatives of all communes[1] (where individuals appear more as consumers than as producers). There is not only a conflict of particular interests within each of these chambers but also among them. Things that would be in the interest of the optimal development of production need not be compatible with an optimal solution of inter-regional relations. (For example opting for maximum industrial output or for optimally efficient investment policy could increase the gap between the developed and underdeveloped regions.) Each chamber would then be able to prevent the unacceptable solutions of the other chamber, by vetoing them, but a mediating authority is obviously necessary to resolve the conflict.

2) In his famous essay on *The Reorganisation of the European Community* Saint-Simon has described the best possible constitution is one in which each question of public interest is always examined first *a priori*, in the light of the common

interest, and then *a posteriori*, in the light of the particular interests of the members of the community. For that purpose, he thought, two distinct agencies are necessary: 'Authority for Common Interests' and 'Authority for Particular or Local Interests'. They would consider matters from different points of view and would have to agree and approve each other's decisions. In order to maintain the balance and resolve the conflicts between them a third, mediating authority seemed to him necessary – he called it a 'Regulating or Moderating Authority'.[2] The basic idea is remarkable, although its concrete form in Saint-Simon is useless for our purpose – he thought that the three institutions exemplifying these three authorities would be the King, the House of Commons and the House of Lords.[3] In the system of self-government the two chambers (of the producers and of the communes) constitute the authority for particular and local interests. A third chamber is needed, composed of the representatives of all citizens, and it would correspond to Saint-Simon's 'Authority for Common Interests'. As a citizen of the global society, an individual would elect a representative who would not be concerned with the particular interests of the enterprise or commune, but with protecting and promoting the common interests of the whole society. Mediation, keeping the balance, and resolution of conflicts, do not require a fourth chamber, but an inter-chamber council carefully selected from the most competent and wisest members of the three chambers.

3) Plato had already expressed in *The Republic* the basic dilemma of each democracy: unlimited craving for freedom could lead to general anarchy. But a demagogue who wins public confidence and strengthens his personal power could easily transform democracy into despotism.[4] The problem.is, then, how to build up a centre with a minimum of necessary (moral and political) authority, how to secure real leadership in the people's interest, but at the same time effectively to block any tendency to acquire a monopoly of political and economic power? The latter will obviously be much easier to achieve if the central unifying authority is not just one person but a small collective, a Praesidium composed of leading figures in all separated powers. Which leads us to the second question:

## 2  How is the separation of powers institutionalised?

Each democratic revolution must produce a new idea for the
separation of powers. One of the greatest achievements of
bourgeois, democratic revolution was the transcendence of
absolute monarchy and the separation of legislative, executive
and judicial powers, with the appropriate mechanism of
checks and balances. The solution was rather simple since the
sphere of political society was separated from the sphere of
civil, economic society; therefore the State was not concerned
with planning, co-ordination and overall control. That is how
the bourgeois State adjusted to a *laissez-faire* competitive,
individualistic, present-oriented society. It is hardly a matter
of chance that Montesquieu ascribed to executive power only
dealing with international relations, and entirely lost sight of
the function of a civil, internal administration.[5] In a modern,
more rational society, at a much higher level of organisation,
in which central political institutions bear basic responsibility
for all socially necessary work, education and social security,
the social decision-making will include new dimensions.

Thus decisions will not be simply expression of interests
compatible with the existing law – they must be based on
knowledge about the existing situation, about the results and
limitations of past policies, the needs of the community, the
beliefs and wants of the population. Such knowledge is
undoubtedly a considerable power. Another power is determination of long-range objectives that guides any enlightened, rational social decision-making. Those who are
responsible for basic goal and project formulation are in fact
most important creators of policies, and hold very important
power.

The experience of all twentieth-century revolutions shows
that those leaders who were responsible for the selection of
cadres were able to dominate trends, to defeat their rivals, and
assume dictatorial power. The cadres policy cannot be that
important in a system of self-government where personnel
cannot simply be nominated, promoted or fired, but must be
democratically elected. Still there is a social need to have a
range of available talent and different kinds of competence for
different functions, to record the achievements and failures of
individuals in their elected public functions, to propose how

the most important functions within a body of self-government should be distributed. *Responsibility for cadres policy* is a decisive power, therefore it should not be in the hands of those who already have other powers – it must be separated.

Finally, there is a need for an *overall control* of the implementation of all policy. This is not only a negative control of legality and formal correctness of all socially necessary activity with the intention of preventing greater social damage, but also a constant social learning from experience, promptly proposing changes in laws, plans and actual policies when they are demanded by new and unexpected factors. Further this is not only control of the practical realisation of the particular interest from the point of view of the common social one, but also control of the common interest whenever it threatens to violate the established rights of the individual and of particular enterprises, communes, regions and branches.

It follows, then, that according to their specific role in the process of a rational decision-making, one should distinguish and separate the following seven powers:

1) *Information* (in the sense of a critical scientific study of the given situation).

2) *Planning* (in the sense of the formulation of basic goals, long-range and short-range projects).

3) *Legislative* (in the classical sense).

4) *Cadres policy* (preparing the proposals of candidates for the most important functions).

5) *Executive* (implementation of accepted policies, basically in the hands of elected representatives, only technically in the hands of experts and professional administration).

6) *Control* (including not only general supervision but also practical intervention).

7) *Judiciary* (in the classical sense).

Institutions for these powers could be councils composed of elected members of the assembly. These councils will run corresponding professional apparatuses: analytical department, planning committees, executive administration, inspection agencies, etc. Each member of the assembly would sit in one of the councils. He would also belong to one of the three chambers as we have seen. The chambers will meet to hear reports and to decide on proposals furnished by the councils.

## 3  Institutions of co-ordination and planning

One of these powers – planning – requires additional discussion, as it is neither theoretically well grounded nor institutionally operationalised.

For a long time planning has been considered by socialists as a necessary and defining characteristic of post-capitalist society. But it turned out that if it was practically implemented (as in the Soviet Union) it became part of a very authoritarian, bureaucratic social structure, whereas if the new society developed in a more democratic, self-governing form (as in Yugoslavia) planning almost disappeared, or was reduced to a mere prognosis of future developments. On the other hand, the trend in the more developed capitalist countries is clearly towards more planning and co-ordination at all levels: within enterprises, national economies, and even in international relations. Such considerations lead to a very superficial and false conclusion, namely that planning 'presupposes an authoritarian State power and that it is incompatible with self-government'. Each of these concepts requires certain distinctions; without them they are source of enormous confusion.

*Planning* could be anything between the commitment to create certain general conditions of social activity, and the formulation of very definite, detailed programmes for each working organisation. *Self-government* does not involve a completely loose, decentralised social organisation allowing a quite important role to the blind forces of the market (as in Yugoslavia in the sixties); if it is fully developed it must replace the State and build up its own central organs. An *authoritarian* State power is, therefore, not simply a strong central power, it is essentialy an *alienated* power, imposing non-internalised tasks from above, compelling to heteronomous behaviour. Each organised society must have a central power and it could be strong in two senses: first, if it enjoys the support of the people; second, if people have freely decided to delegate to it a considerable part of their own power, and have asked it to perform a variety of functions. Thus an authoritarian centre is the stronger the more tasks it imposes on the people; a self-governing centre is the stronger the more tasks it is being given by the people.

These distinctions make it clear that in a developed system of self-government, where the market no longer plays a decisive regulative function, planning is not only possible but necessary. From the will of the people depends whether planning is more or less 'strong' (embracing many activities as central social power's concern) or more or less 'weak' (concentrating on a few activities, and taking care of only very basic among their determinants).

There are four phases of planning:

1) Determination of basic goals.

2) Distribution of responsibility for the realisation of these goals among various levels of self-government.

3) Acceptance of a long-range project.

4) Acceptance of a short-range project.

The determination of the basic social goals is for social praxis what the constitution is for its legal structure. The decision as to which organs of self-government will be responsible for which tasks could follow from the constitution. But it is more concrete and it is better to take them separately than to change the constitution too often.[6] The determination of basic goals and distribution of responsibility for their realisation must be preceded by a sufficiently long debate in mass media, organs of self-government and political organisations. The final drafts prepared by the planning council and endorsed by all three chambers would also have to be accepted by the population through referenda. Whatever weaknesses of the institution of referenda, such important decisions determining all subsequent planning and development must be accepted in a directly democratic way.

A similar synthesis of centralised and decentralised methods will be applied in the preparation and passage of the long-range and short-range projects. In preparing first rough drafts the planning council will have as its starting point the *declaration of basic social goals*, an objective analysis of the situation provided by the information council, an account of the experience in implementing the previous play by the executive council, a critique of previous policy provided by the control council. Again, the preliminary draft is subject to public debate and close scrutiny by all self-governing bodies. These will seek either to adjust to the plan and to reconcile the particular interest which they represent with the common interest expressed by the plan, or else they could condemn the plan as being partial, one-sided, violating their vital interests. In the latter case negotiation is needed. As the result of criticism, the preliminary draft would be revised and a final draft accepted by all three chambers.

Once the plan was passed it could subsequently be revised by the intervention of information and/or control council which would draw attention to any changes in the situation, to unforeseen difficulties, or unnoticed weaknesses in the plan.

## 4   Which are the possible new legal institutions of security and defence?

The existing institution of the State has two opposing functions with respect to the problem of the security and defence of its citizenry. Its police keep a minimum of necessary order and protect the citizen from the criminal activities of others. Its army defends the country from possible aggression from other countries. But the police are increasingly used to harass and oppress idealistic and rebellious youth, exploited, dissatisfied workers, and dissident intellectuals. Ever growing security services collect information about their own people, and actual or possible political opponents of the régime. And the army becomes overwhelmingly a powerful factor of inner political life.

This leads to the following conclusion: the existing forms of the police, security services and army are obsolete. More than ever was the case in the past, these institutions protect by force the particular interests of the ruling oppressive élite. When such an élite no longer exists, these institutions are not needed either. The institutions that replace them will continue to perform the function of defence from criminal activity. But their oppressive function must be abolished and treated itself as a criminal activity, prosecuted by the law and punishable by the court.

What follows is, first, that the number of professional personnel in these institutions as well as the huge expenditure spent on them would be drastically reduced. Second, the people will have to develop their own non-professional, non-oppressive institutions of self-defence. For example, in Yugoslavia there is a large, territorial, civilian defence army ready to offer guerilla resistance in the event of foreign invasion.

The case of invasion by a foreign army is a clear one. All people have a full legal and moral right to defend themselves from violence. Readiness to use that right might decrease the probability of aggression by making the price which the aggressor has to pay too high. On the other hand 'defence of the national interest' is a good example of a vague, general phrase deliberately covering possible abuses.[7]

Another clear case for which some limited degree of intelligence is needed is the activity of the fascists and of the 'Fifth Column' that prepares internally an invasion from outside. What characterises these socially dangerous characters is their readiness to use violence in order to destroy, rather than to protect or promote human rights.

A third case is protection of the individual, of the product of human work, and of the natural environment from criminal activity (the concept of the 'criminal' must be operationally defined by law). In the type of society that is described here criminals would not be condemned as merely vicious, but as persons damaged, needing help in one way or the other. Present-day prisons would be replaced by institutions for treatment, rehabilitation and re-education.

## 5 Political organisations compatible with self-government

Self-government is not compatible with either a one-party or a multi-party system: with the former because it would be dominated by that one political organisation, with the latter because the organisations have the form of a Party.

When there is only one Party which is active, well-organised, interested in increasing its own power, the members of any organ of self-government can be divided into two groups. To the one belong those who participate in the decision-making as independent, unorganised individuals, differing among themselves in some respects, agreeing in others. The second group is constituted by those who come to the meeting as a disciplined organisation which already has its orders of agreed positions on important issues. The latter, even when in a minority, will be able to dominate the scene and to influence decisively all decision-making. It is therefore characteristic that development of self-government in Yugoslavia went together with the transformation of the Party into the League of Communists, which switched from ruling to educating and dissolved its cells in working organisations in order to avoid interference in the decision-making of the workers' councils. When, since 1972, the Party reasserted its right to dominate, and not by patient persuasion but by compulsion, self-government found itself in a serious crisis.

A multi-party system is no solution either. The Party as a specific, historical form of political organisation that is generated in bourgeois society, in most countries only in the second part of the nineteenth century, has serious limitations. Even when a Party is revolutionary it preserves characteristic patterns of domination – hierarchical organisation, authoritarian decision-making, external discipline, ideological forms of consciousness, manipulation of the masses (the object) by the Party (the subject).

When a Party is not (or no longer) revolutionary these domination traits become excellent means to promote the particular interests of the centres of alienated political power.

There is no doubt that in bourgeois society the most powerful Parties express different tendencies and aspirations within the wealthiest social strata.

With the disappearance of such privileged social groups and such centres of alienated political power, the Party, as the form of political organisation, will be transcended. Certainly, many functions that were performed by the Parties will survive, such as articulation of different social needs in the form of practical programmes, mobilisation of supporters for those programmes, political education, control, and the criticism of the implemented policy, taking positions in existing social conflicts, finding ways to their resolution.

A democratic, political life will require a plurality of political organisations: of various clubs, leagues, societies, and unions. They would perform these functions without bosses, large funds, ideologies, or propaganda machineries. A struggle among them would help to clarity the issues, to see the advantages and limitations of their respective positions, to experience the amount of public support for various proposed solutions. In such a way these organisations would inevitably exert a certain pressure on the organs of self-government. But the pressure will come from different directions, and in the absence of force its effect will mainly depend on the strength of arguments and ideas. In fact these types of political organisation will make sense, and will survive only as long as they come up with fresh, attractive ideas which express and articulate the real needs of the largest sections of the population.

While being able to make an impact on organs of self-government by advocating and supporting their ideas, the political organisations do not have a chance of dominating them. One is not elected to a body of self-government because one is a member of a political organisation (although the individual could belong to one and be supported by one). Not Parties, but working organisations, communes, and citizens are represented there. The loyalty of a representative has to go to them. Old-fashioned parliaments, the members of which have to vote according to their Party's faction's order, even when contrary to the interest of their constituency and their own convictions, belong to the past.

## 6 Institutions for the protection of the rights of the minorities and the underprivileged

John Stuart Mill was among the first political scholars who paid great attention to the problems of the minority in a representative democracy. He realised the danger of an intelligent, creative, imaginative, minority being dominated and oppressed by a majority of uneducated, ill-informed, conformist majority. Among the solutions he proposed to prevent this reign of 'collective mediocrity' was one genuinely democratic – the use of proportional representation, that would at least secure the right of the minority to be heard. The other – plural voting in accordance to intelligence – was obviously élitist. In a participatory democracy without monopoly of power, without strong conditioning of conformist behaviour, and with better opportunities of education for all, majority and minority would not so often differ substantially in intelligence, knowledge or creativity. Furthermore, if important decisions are preceded by debate in the organs of self-government, and if free media always offer an opportunity to express criticism, to explain and justify one's viewpoint, and engage in dialogue with opposing viewpoints then, rather than be simply buried beneath a huge mass of voters, more intelligent and knowledgeable ones will have a relatively better chance to influence and persuade them. The more democracy is reduced to a mere right to vote, the greater is the danger for creative minorities. The more democracy involves participation and dialogue, the greater influence and higher social status of the naturally gifted. In fact, when all social institutions are removed that produce present-day political and economic inequalities (the privileges of birth, capital, the Church and the State) differences in natural abilities will continue to give rise to inequalities in social status and power of influence – the problem quite opposite to the one cited by Mill.

In participatory democracy the problem of the minority will be much more the consequence of differences in interests than of differences of intelligence. There are at least three ways of protecting the minority.

First, the institution of self-managing agreement. Many social matters will have to be solved by agreement of all partners, rather than by the application of a law or by the majority vote. For example a Yugoslav university is such a loose association that in a number of basic, specific issues something can be decided only when all faculties agree. On such issues it never comes to the vote. Negotiations involving all kinds of pressures and concessions are followed until a compromise solution is reached. Naturally the size of each partner does not count.

Second, the classical power of veto. In certain top institutions, on certain vital issues, a minority can prevent an unfavourable decision by vetoing it. For example, each of the eight Yugoslav federal units has the right to veto proposed decisions concerning federal economic collaboration.

Third, when, from the point of view of the unity of society, it is essential to treat each particular interest as equally important in spite of its size, it will be given an equal number of votes. Thus each national republic in Yugoslavia sends thirty representatives into one of the two chambers of the federal assembly dealing with defence, with the changes in the constitution, the borders of the federation, its budget and other sensitive issues. Whether an institution of this type is introduced depends on the basic conception of a community. If the community is an association of groups (nationalities, or national republics) it follows that each group should be equally represented, whatever its size. But if a community is an association of human individuals (citizens, producers) then by applying the rule described above some minority groups would be over-protected and the rights of the individual damaged. When two national groups send an equal number of representatives to the assembly, and one group is ten times smaller than the other, it follows that its citizens are considerably better represented.

When none of these three rules is applicable, a minority out-voted on an important issue and convinced that the decision is wrong must have the following way to protect its dignity and integrity in a sane, democratic society: it would have to show its respect for the will of majority and refrain from obstructing its practical realisation. But far from simply conforming (demanded by the principle of 'democratic centralism') the minority would either be able to leave the given organisation or community (which would be respected in an honest act by the majority) or it would have the right to revive the issue as soon as attempts to implement the decision of the majority in practice furnish new arguments against it.

There is another group of cases where the global society has to pay special attention to a vulnerable but important particular interest. Differing from the case where a group is weak because it is small, here it is weak because it is underdeveloped, because, during a long period in the past, it was treated as a politically and economically inferior part of society. The backward ones could be a majority and still not yet fully be able to exercise their new rights. Or, as the consequence of centuries of oppression, a whole half of the population – women – continue to behave as second-class citizens even if they have already achieved legal equality. The most unfortunate case is when the underdeveloped are also a minority – for example the blacks or the Indians in the USA.

The least that can and must be done urgently is the provision of legal equality.

Another relatively simple measure is the giving of the largest possible political and cultural autonomy wherever possible, for example for national and racial minorities.

These two measures prevent further oppression. But the main problem is to reduce and bridge the existing gap. That requires a number of new institutions.

The basic one is a federal fund for aid to the underdeveloped regions. The advanced regions would pay special contributions into such a fund, which would then allocate aid according to need.

There should be analogous funds for the improvement of the education of minorities that are underprivileged and underdeveloped in the present society. Merely building up special educational institutions for them or opening the gates of the existing ones under formally equal conditions would involve considerable difficulties. Separate education would probably remain inferior in quality and formal equality of admittance into better schools would only reinforce the existing real inequality. What is therefore needed is all kinds of 'catch-up' programmes and facilities – especially for underdeveloped minorities – that offer opportunities of an accelerated education and cultural development.

One of the most complex problems is the liberation of women from their present inferior social status. This is not only the problem of legal equality, or of formal education, or of working opportunities. Essentially this is the problem of overcoming the division of work into domestic and public spheres and of the whole ideology that fixes women to the role of housewife and mother. The least that can be done at the institutional level is the creation of all kinds of services and facilities that help overcome the drudgery of the housework.

## 7   Institutions for the protection of citizens' rights

In all present-day societies the individual is insufficiently protected against abuse by the State and powerful social organisations. Even in the most liberal system, there is little that a person can do against the violation of his rights, or against decisions and policies of the State and big corporations that damage his interests. He can write to his congressman or senator, or can organise a citizen's committee, complain in the media or even sue the State. This is quite impressive in comparison with a totalitarian system where the individual is completely at the mercy of powerful bureaucratic machinery and the organs of 'public order'. The people's representative depends to some extent on his voters, the media are free to criticise the government, and the courts are free to prosecute the State; a great democratic revolution was needed to achieve these freedoms.

But in a capitalist world most of these freedoms are only a matter of legal possibility. Justice is expensive. The individual has a better chance of real protection from his representative only when the latter no longer needs the support of powerful financial groups and Party bosses to be elected, and when he no longer regards his office as merely a step up the ladder of social hierarchy. His voice has a better chance of being heard in the mass media only when the latter lose their present commercial and ideological function. And the courts will only become less organs of punishment and more institutions of citizens' protection when the function of the lawyer, analogously to the role of the doctor, is socialised. Like the sick person who cannot seek medical help because he cannot afford it, so the individual whose rights have been violated cannot get legal advice because he lacks financial means. This condition is overcome only when society builds up a network of institutions (at all levels of social organisation) for the protection of human rights. These institutions would not only inform the individual about his rights and give free legal advice, in addition they would – like Scandinavian ombudsmen – have the power to undertake all kinds of fact-finding investigations, to intervene directly in favour of the wronged individual and to demand urgent solutions of issues of more general importance.

It is a great irony that today the whole issue of human rights is so badly neglected, both in theory and in practice, by the adherents of the man who in 1847 in the conclusion of his *Manifesto* said that in the new society 'free development of each individual will be the condition of the free development of all society'.[8]

## Notes

1 In Yugoslavia the latter is the Chamber of Nationalities, as the country is a

federation of six national republics and two autonomous regions of different size and level of development, so that national relations remain a very important and sensitive issue.

2  Henri de Saint-Simon, *Social Organisation, The Science of Man and Other Writings*, Harper Torchbooks, Harper & Row, New York, 1964, pp. 40–1.

3  *Ibid*, p. 42–3.

4  Plato, *The Republic*, Book VII.

5  Montesquieu, *The Spirit of the Laws*, Book XI, ch. 6.

6  Change of conditions – such as energy crises, awareness of ecological and demographic dangers – would require changes in priorities of goals and distribution of responsibility, both without change of the constitution.

7  For example, US allegedly 'defended' its national interest in Vietnam, and is again ready to defend it in the Middle East. The Soviet Union claims to have 'defended' its national interest by invading Hungary in 1956, Czechoslovakia in 1968 and Afghanistan in 1979.

8  Marx and Engels, The *Manifesto of the Communist Party*.

# 8 Culture and Morality in Socialism

## 1 Cultural praxis

The present division of society into a political sphere in which an individual is subordinated to the State, and the civil sphere in which he is free to pursue his egoistic interests will be replaced by a distinction between the *public life* regulated by democratically adopted communal rules, and *personal life* regulated only by ethical rules and by autonomous, individual intentions. Once the only social obligation – work – is met, an individual will freely decide how much he wants to be secluded and how much he will participate in the activities of various communities – working, political, cultural, sporting, entertaining.

An increasing amount of human life will tend to take place outside the public sphere of the global society, in smaller, freely elected communities and in individual, spontaneous, self-expressive activities.

Humanistic socialism is anything but a uniform, highly regulated society of worker ants. It is a more personalised society than any in human history – certainly more than liberal bourgeois society, in which real individual freedom is greatly restricted by the uncontrollable forces of the State and the market. A person in a humanistic socialist society is not only a unique being but also, in contrast to the selfish, isolated, bourgeois individual, a communal being, deeply concerned about the condition of others.

There are two factors that account for this process of progressive liberation from the necessities of global life. First, the amount of obligatory public work decreases with the rigid increase of its productivity. In all historical variability and uncertainty one constant may be reliably established and extrapolated: growth of knowledge, increasing wealth of scientific information, progressive development of productive forces. It follows that the same level of satisfaction of human needs of the same number of people will be achieved with progressively decreasing amount of working time. People still work insanely long hours because production is geared to profit and consumerism. Even in the initial stages of the new society emerging from an insufficiently developed bourgeois society some excessive work may be needed to eliminate material misery and satisfy the elementary needs to all members of that society.

But then, instead of wasteful exponential growth of material output a switch toward higher-level cultural needs becomes possible, and indeed necessary. It becomes possible because under given social conditions there is no longer any social force that has any interest or the power to push toward a surplus of material goods, and the creation of artificial needs for them. The switch toward culture becomes necessary for ecological reasons, and as a consequence of a radically changed anti-consumerist consciousness. The anti-consumerism that we are witnessing today, especially among youth, is still inconsistent. Excessive consumption of material goods has been replaced by excessive consumption of *cultural* and *pseudo-cultural* goods. But the point is not to consume cultural goods (often of doubtful value) passively but to take an active part in creating culture, to take part in performing cultural activities in the same way in which one will freely participate in the political process, in meaningful communication of all sorts, and in play and love.

There are three basic conditions for such an expansion of cultural praxis. Top quality cultural performances ought to become increasingly free. Society should provide the necessary facilities for cultural activities: theatres, musical instruments, exhibition halls, printing equipment. And most important of all, all education should be radically re-oriented. What is nowadays the main goal of education – the preparation for a specialised role in the division of socially necessary labour – will increasingly become a matter of secondary importance. The primary goal of education becomes self-understanding, discovery of one's creative potential, preparation of a basic life-project, building corresponding necessary skills for autonomous self-development and self-expressing activities. This does not mean that everybody will become an Einstein or a Bartók. But one will have a chance of becoming what one is by disposition.

From the institutional point of view the following changes are needed:

a) transformation of existing schools into complex institutions embracing not only classrooms but also laboratories, workshops, gardens, studios, concert halls, theatres and sports grounds – some of which already exist in Western universities and propaganda oriented Eastern palaces for the 'pioneers' (members of children establishment organisations);

b) free education for all, and increasing participation in decision-making from early childhood;

c) creation of numerous cultural institutions in which non-professional artists, scholars, lecturers may freely perform;

d) expansion of continuing adult education which will offer knowledge, skills, creative hobbies, and a chance to prepare for different kinds of work.

## 2   The new status of mass media

If any particular interest dominates the mass media, it dominates the whole society. Where television, radio and national newspapers are in the hands of big business it is easy for the bourgeois Parties to rule and to keep a wasteful economy going by imposing ever new artificial consumer needs on the population. Where mass media are fully controlled by political bureaucracy, people are utterly confused about the true nature of the system in which they live, and are ready to accept it as the natural or even optimal form of social life.

Thus in oppressive class societies the function of mass media is less to inform and educate, and much more to manipulate, brainwash, distract from real problems and make possible a rule by consent of the apathetic, silent majority.

In a democratic classless society mass media can become what they potentially are: powerful means of disseminating real information, of public communication. They are absolutely necessary for the efficient functioning of self-government. It would be foolish not to recognise that the decisions taken by the organs of self-government may be inadequate, biased, wrong, irrational. They would be less so if, in the given community, there is powerful, critical public opinion and a constant dialogue about the most important public matters. It should be inconceivable to take decisions on such matters without previous debates in which the various points of view of individuals and organisations could be freely expressed, explored and mediated. But then it follows that the ground on which someone will have the opportunity to be represented in a mass medium is not whether he bought time or space, or whether he belongs to the group that owns or controls that medium, but whether he can say something meaningful and socially relevant.

Therefore mass media must not be monopolised by any particular interest – private corporations, the Parties, the Church, the State. They must not be privately-owned and profit-oriented as in capitalist countries, nor State-owned as in State-socialism of the Soviet type, nor commercial, self-governing in material matters while firmly controlled by bureaucracy in ideological matters, as in socialism of the Yugoslav type. In each of these cases information is grossly distorted and free circulation of ideas arrested.

The optimal form of organisation and regulation of the legal status of mass media that would solve their material problems without diminishing their freedom and without pushing them into market competition, would probably be a self-governing community of mass media, supported through the annual allocation of a fixed percentage of the national income. The community would be run by an assembly constituted by the representatives of all newspapers, broadcasting and television stations, and by the delegated representatives of consumers and the global society. Each mass medium would, of course, have its own workers' council. Their policy would naturally be to restore the informative, communicative and educational function of mass media and to offer equal opportunity to express different ideas and viewpoints. One viewpoint could be more reasonable and more in agreement with explicit social goals than another but its confrontation with other viewpoints will offer the best chance of winning public support, and be internalised rather than imposed by the force of repetition.

## 3   New institutions for a new culture

The legal status of scientific institutes, schools and universities, publishing houses, theatres, concert halls, picture galleries and film producers would be comparable to that of mass media. A network of self-governing councils with an assembly on the top of the pyramid would be responsible for educational, scientific and cultural policy. Although some of the institutions from this whole field could have their own income – to the extent to which books, films, records, theatre and concert performances, lectures, applied science services keep being treated, at least partly, as commodities – they must be partly subsidised to avoid both élitism and commercialisation, and the ultimate goal must be Malraux's *dictum: culture must be free*. New social conditions will create possibilities for a new Renaissance in the arts and sciences, for an epoch of immense flourishing of culture. The present profound crises of culture, manifesting itself on the one hand in gross abuse of science and technology for destructive, wasteful and propaganda purposes, in widespread technicism and élitism, and on the other hand in popular rejection of culture as a bourgeois phenomenon, in cultural nihilism (anti-theatre, anti-paintings, anti-university), in various forms of counter-culture has its roots in a general climate of decay, generated by unbearable social inequalities, and more and more meaningless aggression used to preserve them.

In a society characterised by *equality of condition* for each individual to realise his full potential the very basic cultural task will be to discover talent wherever it exists and give it the chance to develop. This will profoundly change the nature of all education and consequently of all educational institutions. New schools will primarily have to offer appropriate facilities and extend the educator's help to each individual to discover his best creative capacities. Thus they will establish the role of mediator between the accumulated culture of the past and the present generation's experiences and needs. Only then, will they have to prepare individuals for definite roles and tasks in the division of socially necessary work – the last, and also the least, because with an increase of efficiency the sphere of socially necessary work will require less and less amounts of time and energy.

# 4 Basic moral values from the standpoint of an ideal community of praxis

The vision of an ideal community of praxis, which tends to

realise fully all that is distinctly human in history, constitutes the ethical ground in our present alienated society.

In this ethics the idea of *summum bonum* – the highest good – is more distant from reality than in other non-religious ethical systems. Most of these systems coincide with an already existing morality, and are compatible with given social arrangements, no matter how unjust. For example *utilitarianism* from Aristippus to Epicurus and from there to Bentham, Mill, Sidgwick and Moore did not really challenge the established society, whatever it was. Seeking pleasure and calculating how to achieve it is an invariant in customary human behaviour, and even when these are achieved to the maximum quantity of highest quality for a maximum number of individuals, it remains a moral issue within a given social framework. The same holds for ethics of duty, whether of Kant, Ross or Pritchard. The sense of duty is formal and directs different people in divergent ways. The apologist of a most oppressive system may be prepared to will that the maxims of his actions should become universal law.

Dewey's pragmatic ethics, with its emphasis on continued growth in the sense of an increasing variety of needs and harmony in their satisfaction, clashes with traditional, static morality, but expresses quite well the ideological needs of any modern industrial society.

Examples of ethical theories that involve rebellious elements but in a harmless individualistic form are Stoic and existentialist ethics. They offer moral solutions to individuals in unbearable external conditions. One expresses the ideal of spiritual independence and serenity that can be achieved by reduction of desires and withdrawal from the world's competition and conflict. The other commits one to absolute freedom, disregard of all bonds and imposed constraints, even at the risk of death. They retain their validity for individuals in exceptional situations, but are essentially escapist.

Humanist ethics based on the notion of praxis projects an idea of *eudaimonia* – good life – which requires radical, social transformation. That each human individual should be able to live as a being of praxis involves a very revolutionary moral demand of economic, political and cultural liberation, of maximum possible creativity, of social solidarity. Most of what various ethical theories praised as basic virtues and ultimate ends finds its place and a new meaning within this context. Plato's virtues – wisdom, courage, temperance and justice – are no longer related to a contemplative reason but to a rational activity of shaping the world according to human capacities and needs. As Butler noticed in theory and John Stuart Mill in his own life, very little pleasure can be achieved when pleasure becomes an end in itself; it is only a by-product that accompanies attainment of ends other than pleasure. Stoic peace of soul and spiritual independence is of limited value when it goes with a poor life devoid of almost all content; it becomes an entirely different value at a much higher level of material and cultural development and of social emancipation. Then it will be attained by renouncing dominating power and the accumulation of material wealth, by aspiring to a free, productive life in a healthy harmonious social environment. In this context freedom is much more than mere freedom of thought, or a desperate act of choice of an uprooted, isolated existence; it is a way of life that recognises needs and the interests of other individuals and society as a whole, that within such inevitable constraints creates ever new possibilities, chooses autonomously from them, and brings the chosen project into being.

The idea of a *natural* moral law, in the sense given to it by Hugo Grotius, as a set of rules based on the universal nature of man, plays an important role in all humanist ethics; however it requires a dynamic re-interpretation. Since human nature evolves in history and is exemplified in a different, unique way in each individual, moral goodness is not an abstract static concept. Dynamic concepts of traditional ethics, such as self-realisation and self-perfection are therefore indispensable, although they get a new meaning. The self is not an isolated, selfish individual, but essentially a communal being, therefore *self-realisation* means bringing to life those potential capacities which do not only affirm individual interests, but also promote social good. *Self-perfection* means the development of rational, creative capacities rather than a spiritual ascent to God, as in mediaeval ethics. However there is one great idea in the Christian tradition which is superior to the abstract and uniform treatment of man by many subsequent rationalists and humanists. This is the idea that moral goodness is in doing one's best with one's specific natural endowments and in given circumstances. This principle of individuation, or of personalism, has rarely been respected in traditional ethics which, in a rather formal way, emphasised general principles, rules and duties. Even Hegel, who in his critique of Kant's formalism required a concern about content of ethical judgements, thought that content came from the customs, norms and laws of the particular society in which the agent lived. This obviously leads to moral conformism, and that is why Hegel saw the highest expression of morality in the State.

Here we have a dilemma between an extreme *subjectivist* conception of morality resting on self-interest and self-preservation of the individual agent, and an opposite *objectivist* view of morality as subordinated to God, or to the State (which itself is an objective form of Absolute Spirit), or to an abstraction of social good. In order to resolve that dilemma we must assume that man is both a unique person and a social being, that he feels genuinely concerned about certain general needs, without ever surrendering his personal autonomy and integrity. As a result of socialisation an individual internalises the values of his community; unless he grows together, communicates and interacts with other members, he never develops any moral consciousness. However as a being of praxis, man has a unique capacity of *critical self-consciousness*, therefore he can come to believe that there are certain general limitations in the prevailing morality, and that he should not always conform to its norms. He may be wrong and become a social outcast. But he may also be right and contribute by his deviant moral behaviour to the emergence of a new superior morality.

New morality lives for some time only in the praxis of most developed individuals, or in the form of ethical theory. It prevails and begins to be lived by the masses in times of profound social crisis when the whole social fabric and ideology of the ruling élite collapses, and the need for social restructuring is felt irresistably.

New morality rejects some traditional norms or weakens them in the sense that they lose their former high place in the hierarchy of values. Humanist ethics that emphasises *being* rather than *having* will no longer give a high priority to the protection of property or of other characteristically bourgeois institutions. It will no longer be considered right to kill in the defence of property, to compel the repayment of debts, when these are unjust and involve leaving children hungry, to keep promises even when they have been forced by manipulation and repression, to stay married without love, to acquire wealth without work, to discriminate against certain people because they belong to a different class, sex, race or religion.

Traditional socialist elements in this new morality are demands that each member of the community ought to contribute his share of socially necessary work, and that all social goods should be distributed according to the amount and quality of this contribution, but also according to specific individual needs. Such norms exclude both exploitation and privilege and any distribution according to inherited social status or property. Socialist ethics has also always with good reason insisted on a principle of solidarity, mutual support and aid to the weak, poor, old and ill. However there is a void in traditional socialist ethics which must be filled: neglect of moral issues concerning personal self-determination, integrity and inner harmony. Since society cannot be fully emancipated without emancipation of the individual, a true socialist morality must allow the possibility that an individual or a particular community may be morally right against any existing organisation, institution or society as a whole. Praxis transcends any established order, whenever that order becomes too narrow for creative innovation. Therefore moral self-determination is more than a mere freedom of will, it involves the moral right of the individual to go beyond social constraints and create new possibilities, and also involves not only an autonomous act of choice but action according to choice.

From such an ethical standpoint personal integrity is placed very highly on the scale of moral values, in contrast to the duplicity of most prevailing morality which divorces thought, will and action. An obvious example may be found in the ethics of Hobbes who adopted Christian moral rules, but considered it a folly to act according to them as all people are selfish, and so are not likely to follow them. The possibility of such morality depends, then, on State authority and the law which enforce the rules. Once Hobbes' assumption of the anti-social nature of man is abandoned, there is no longer a need to be a beast during the week and a saint on Sundays, and to support a coercive State machinery in order to force others into observing an indispensable minimum of morality. An individual must take the risk and live his moral philosophy – only then will he satisfy his genuine need for full personal integrity, for harmony between his beliefs, verbal utterances and overt acts.

Obviously one can resolve inner conflicts and restore integrity in different ways within a continuum, between egoism and altruism. The optimal solution is such a self-affirmation which also involves a concern for the well-being of others. This principle follows analytically from the very concept of praxis; it excludes both the giving away of one's life, and abuse and disregard of others'. It does not demand love for everybody, but recognises a basic respect and sympathy for another human being and a genuine concern about his needs.

## 5 The phenomenon of moral disintegration in post-capitalist societies

The existence of a sufficient number of morally integrated personalities is one of the necessary conditions for the realisation of all other moral values of a socialist society. The complete abolition of all concealed forms of exploitation, the creation of equal social conditions for the full development of each individual, help to the weak and underdeveloped to solve their initial material and other difficulties, genuine distribution of products according to work, solidarity among individuals and social groups – all these values of the new society can be materialised only in so far as they become internalised in the total behaviour of an increasing number of individuals, instead of being accepted only in a declarative and inconsistent way. The lack of integrity, the mass phenomenon of split personalities, indicates that society is passing through a period of crisis, that one morality is disintegrating and that another has not yet taken root. It may also mean that the society cherishes illusions about its own morality, that its normative moral consciousness is in more or less sharp conflict with the actual standards of behaviour, and that disintegrative social factors prevail over integrative ones.

Some Marxists explain the negative phenomena in socialist societies (such as hypocrisy, duplicity, discrepancy between public and private life of an individual, between his thoughts and actions) as the result of the remnants of bourgeois or petty-bourgeois consciousness. It may well be true that the lack of integrity in many individuals whose characters have been formed in the old society is the result of their incapacity to internalise the values of the new morality, no matter how great their efforts are to conform to its requirements. However, there are also undoubtedly many cases of moral disintegration in individuals educated in the new society, and even in some active participants in the initial stages of the revolutionary movement. Such processes of moral deformation and degradation cannot be satisfactorily explained away by the all too simple scheme of 'the remnants of old in the heads of people'. They demand a radical, critical analysis of the new conditions and new social factors which produce such undesirable moral consequences.

While the individual deliberately subordinates himself to the collective, and postpones the satisfaction of many of his personal needs, which is characteristic in the early stages of the socialist revolution, while his life in the present experiences its profound sense only in so far as it leads to an ideal State in the future, it is relatively easy to achieve a very high degree of coherence between word and deed, norm and actual behaviour. Life in the future inspires a feeling of youth, vitality, hope, unlimited confidence in history, in leaders and companions. The anticipation of shared ultimate goals, close cooperation, a considerable degree of closeness of the group in relation to all external factors, the acceptance of specific rules, symbols, rituals, forms of communication peculiar to the members of the group – all these create an exceptionally high solidarity within its framework.

By the time this revolutionary group becomes the leading political force and its moral values come to be the leading morality of the whole society, many conditions will have profoundly changed and some unsuspected contradictions will have arisen.

One of the essential changes is that the satisfaction of individual needs on a much higher level than the one which was acceptable and considered natural in the period of the revolutionary struggle for power can no longer be delayed. Besides, there is the policy of material incentives for work which is necessary for a long period of socialist development and which becomes especially important in the initial limited forms of a system of self-management, with its strong emphasis on the initiative and responsibility of each producer. In many individuals such conditions bring about a change in the character of motivation and a transfer from general and collective ends, to personal and egoistic ones. On the other hand, a socialist society must make efforts to develop collective consciousness, to propagate general socialist goals and ideals. It continues to demand personal risks and sacrifices; This is a contradictory social situation: many of those practices which are being criticised at political meetings and in the media do not clash with the existing laws and economic instruments. The protests and criticisms become rather declarative and formalistic, which leads to a characteristic duality – between paying lip-service to general socialist values at appropriate places and times, and a purely pragmatic behaviour on all other occasions.

Individual needs in an insufficiently developed society will tend to be primarily needs for material objects rather than intellectual and cultural aspirations. This fact gives rise to a specific form of the contradiction mentioned above: while developing its productive forces society tends to reproduce a type of *homo consumens*, well-known from highly developed capitalist society, but at the same time it still preaches modesty and, at least verbally, sticks to Marx's humanist ideal of man who wants to *be* and not just to *have*.

In the initial phase of a revolutionary movement the practice of an individual is rather simple: ultimate goals are very general and the question of the modes of their realisation remains to be solved, while immediate goals, i.e. criticism and abolition of the institutions of the existing society, are predominantly negative and insufficiently clear. In later developments the revolutionary practice of individuals and the whole social community become ever more complex and multi-valued. Each new step in the process of human liberation is a new negation of the initial rigid determinism, opening new objective possibilities, and a growth of the number of alternatives from which to choose. This choice is not always purely rational, and does not always sufficiently take into account the general interest of the social community as a whole; national, regional, professional group-interests begin to play an increasing role. One of the difficulties is that it is no longer easy for an individual to know what is really in the general social interest. In the conditions of an authoritarian and bureaucratic centralism, an individual is confronted with just one coherent apparatus, which claims to speak in the name of the whole society. The attitude of an individual toward this unique centre of power depends on how much he is convinced that this power genuinely represents the society, or perhaps just a bureaucratic oppression group, or anything in between. So his moral situation is quite clear in this respect.

However, at a higher and more democratic level of socialist society, where the process of withering away of the State has already begun, followed by a growth of initiative and relative freedom of resistance of local institutions to the central organs of power, an individual is confronted with a whole series of intermediate centres of power which all claim to speak in the name of society, but which differ in ranging degrees, or even clash among themselves. A specially unfavourable case is when we have a polycentrism without a corresponding decrease in the amount of alienated political power.

The question what is the social interest? can no longer be decided by simply endorsing or resisting the official line of the central bodies; very often there is no longer just one such line. By now the dogma that the highest authority is always right has already been abandoned. Now the individual himself must find out what is in the general social interest. Before he knows that, he is not able to decide whom and what it would be morally right to support or resist.

In such conditions the degree of moral responsibility of an individual has been greatly increased, which implies an increase in the number of conflicting situations which bring to test his moral integrity. An individual now plays many different and often conflicting roles in the society. He is no longer a predominantly political being whose other activities are moulded both in form and content according to the accepted political goals. The evolution of socialist society has so far clearly manifested a tendency towards progressive emancipation of the various roles which an individual plays in society from his political functions. While engaged in economic, scientific, artistic or any other sphere of social life, especially in his private life, an individual feels less and less bound to act according to any external, strictly political standards. Under certain conditions there is no doubt that the emancipation from the hegemony of politics is a progressive process. The monism of politics in the early stages of revolutionary struggle is obviously the consequence of a very limited historical situation: the conditions of human life can be decisively changed only by a political action. The very fact that all other spheres of social consciousness, such as economics, science, philosophy and arts, have to be subordinated to politics shows that politics is still a sphere of alienation, a sphere of a partial human existence. Therefore in a society which tends toward disalienation of man and human practice it is necessary to supersede the hegemony of politics and to replace abstract external and onesided political standards by new concrete standards specific to each sphere of human creativity and derivable from fundamental human values.

However the question arises *whether the disintegration of the initial totality of social consciousness achieved on the basis of the subordination to politics means at the same time an integration of the social consciousness on a new higher level.*

The main factor which causes the disintegration of many personalities is the fact that in social practice, in various forms of social consciousness, contradictory norms and contradictory criteria of evaluation take more and more ground, and we are not even sufficiently aware of that fact because the existing institutions still preserve the illusion of unity secured by politics in the old sense.

In so far as by 'politics' we mean both laying down immediate social goals and all decision-making which leads to the realisation of these goals, there is no doubt that it will greatly condition the character of global social consciousness. But if politics plays an extraordinarily great role, and if it lacks integrity, it is difficult to speak about an integrated homogeneous social consciousness. As a consequence, a person living in such a society will suffer mutually incompatible pressures in various aspects of social life and will be tempted to show a different face when playing each of his different social roles.

This happens especially when politics suffers from two of its classical defects. One is the gap between proclaimed principles and programmes and their practical realisation. The other is the traditional cleavage between politics as a whole and all other forms of social consciousness – morality, science, philosophy, law and the arts.

In a post-capitalist society politics still has these defects and retains them for a long time. Many proclaimed ends and principles are only being incompletely realised, e.g. the rule of the workers, equal conditions for work and development of each individual, distribution of products according to work, rotation of leaders, bridging the gap between intellectual and physical work, abolition of the differences between developed and backward regions, etc. This discrepancy between programme and practice, declarations and deeds, is not solely the result of objective difficulties. It would be hard to deny that in many State-socialist countries material conditions for a much greater role of every individual producer in social decision-making have already been created.

However, politics is still separated from and even opposed to other forms of social consciousness. It is little founded on reliable scientific knowledge about given social situations and objective tendencies of its change. Efforts to integrate politics within a broader philosophical context are non-existent or superficial. In addition to law, politics often has a pragmatic attitude – every law can be so interpreted as to be suitably applied. Especially serious is the divergence between politics and morality. To the extent to which the principle of success and of efficiency plays a decisive role in politics, it is inevitably going to conflict with the moral norms. Many Marxists nowadays do not hesitate to admit that politics cannot be both successful and morally flawless. Because, as they would say, following Sartre's hero in *Les mains sales*, one cannot keep one's hands clean when the question is to be or not to be, and when one fights against an enemy who has no moral scruples and who uses every means at his disposal. Such a justification of the discrepancy between politics and morality rests either on a lack of understanding of the historical character of morality, or on the bureaucratic deformations of politics (or both).

The first is in question when morality is conceived as a set of universal, absolute norms of human behaviour. In fact the concept of a morally good action refers to a given historical context. That which otherwise, and in a different situation, would not be moral might be morally right in the struggle against an enemy who has no moral scruples and who is ready to use every means at his disposal. For example, from the nature of a war it depends whether it would be morally right or wrong to take part in it.

When morality is conceived as a historical phenomenon whose norms have to be constituted and interpreted only in specific historical conditions, the amoralism of politics in a post-capitalist society cannot but be a consequence of its bureaucratisation. The tendencies of bureaucratisation are the essential factor which destroys the integrity of consciousness of a social community and which indirectly undermines the moral integrity of each individual.

1) Bureaucracy tends to keep and preserve a monopoly on the function of ruling essential social process. Political decision-making thus becomes the monopoly of a particular social group. As a particular profession, politics becomes isolated from all other forms of social consciousness. In order to overcome this isolation it tends to subordinate them. This leads to the following contradictions: on the one hand, the complexity of various goals of socialist society demands the emancipation of culture from the external control of politics; on the other hand, politics tends to preserve its controlling and directing function as a particular profession, as an external, institutionalised social power, and not as the political consciousness and political activity of the producers in the realm of culture themselves.

It is not only the case that a person engaged in scientific, artistic, philosophical or any other cultural activity feels a conflict between political demands and the generally accepted norms in the field in which he is active, he also feels a conflict between what he both as a producer and as a political being knows would be the politically optimal course of action and what comes as a directive from an external political body which is ignorant of the concrete situation and of the specific features of the activity in question.

2) Bureaucracy pretends to rule in the name of the working masses. It makes a great effort to create this illusion. Therefore it proclaims many goals which correspond to the needs and demands of the masses. But it is legitimate to speak about a bureaucracy just in so far as this ruling group also has its own particular interests which can be secured only if, in practice, it

constantly deviates from its publicly announced principles and programmes. What follows is a wide gap between norm and reality, especially concerning democratisation of social life. Bureaucracy cannot both allow genuine election and the replacement of all organs of power, and survive as a particular social group. Therefore it must resolutely resist progressive democratisation of socialist society while pretending to accept it.

3) Bureaucracy uses its power of disposing with objectified labour in order to expropriate a part of the surplus value in the form of various privileges. In a society in which the abolition of exploitation is considered one of the fundamental values, and the standard of living is still relatively low, the awareness of this fact might really have destructive moral consequences, because a new morality cannot be born spontaneously, no matter how the revolutionary *avant garde* behaves. Therefore political leaders in a socialist society will either fight against the tendencies towards bureaucratisation in society and in themselves, and in such a case they will remain the carriers of new, more humane moral values, or they will choose to demand that their past revolutionary services be abundantly paid off, and in that case they no longer have the right to be considered a revolutionary, *avant garde* and progressive social force.

The conclusion is that not all manifestations of hypocrisy, discrepancy between the public and private life of an individual, between norms and actual behaviour, manifestations of duplicity and multiplicity in the behaviour of the same individual can be explained by the assumption of the 'remnants of old bourgeois mentality in the heads of people'. Some are the effect of the following disintegrative factors:

1) *An excessive urge to satisfy individual material needs*, although productivity is still so low that only a minority can reach an essentially higher level of the gratification of those needs. In such conditions the character of motivation can be changed and the individual may suffer a moral regression.

2) *Simple dispersion of alienated political power into a greater number of centres* as a substitute for a process of gradual disappearance of professional political power. The total amount of alienated political power can even be increased in this way. At any rate the multiplication of political centres might lead to the

multiplication of dilemmas in the practical choices to be made.

3) *The separation and isolation of various particular spheres of social consciousness*, the formation of different and often opposite criteria of evaluation for each of them.

4) *The tendency of conservation of politics as a partial, professional and essentially pragmatic activity* which does not hesitate to be amoral in order to reach maximum of efficiency.

5) *The existence of a bureaucratic élite* which, in a concealed form, tends to realise its own particular interests (monopoly of political power, material privileges) while at the same time rationalising its role, and creating various illusions about itself.

From this analysis it follows that if progressive forces in a post-capitalist society want to create favourable social conditions for the growth of healthy, integrated personalities they must fight all sorts of privileges, all attempts to preserve the alienation of economic and political power, to perpetuate politics as a particular sphere of social consciousness and a particular profession.

Or, if we want to express what is essential in just one sentence: *moral integrity of individuals in a post-capitalist society is decisively determined by the degree of its debureaucratisation.*

# 9   Possibilities of an Evolution Toward Democratic Socialism

In Czechoslovakia in 1968 Soviet tanks put an end to a process which, in all probability and for the first time in history, would have shown the world what democratic socialism was like. The collapse of Stalinism in Czechoslovakia had alarmed most conservative bureaucratic forces to such an extent that an international 'Holly Alliance' of bureaucracy was created in order to preserve so called 'real socialism' by all available forms of pressure and violence. The alliance did not stop at brutally intervening in individual cases, but has since developed an entirely new theory of collective sovereignty which allows the first 'real socialist' State to pursue its particular super-power political interests under the ideological guise of 'proletarian internationalism'.

These interests are differentiated in different parts of the world. Within the socialist 'camp' the basic goal is to preserve the existing power structure with total State control of all social life. In the belt of States surrounding the camp, the professed objective of Soviet policy is to support and promote the victory of friendly régimes. This involves hostility not only towards an alliance of any of these régimes with another super-power, but also towards any social change which is not inspired by the Soviet model. In the Third World, liberation movements are supported both politically and materially, and it is true that without such aid some among those movements would have been crushed. On the other hand, every means is used – with varying success – to influence the ideology of those movements and to influence the establishment of the new, victorious régime. Finally, in the advanced capitalist countries, the only accepted political force is a party as close to Lenin's paradigm as possible; and the only endorsed strategy of social change is that of a violent revolution of the Bolshevik type – which is 'realistically' postponed for an indefinite future. What underlies these apparent differences of approach is a rigid and totally unrealistic identification of all real socialism in the world with the Soviet model. The consequence is that contemporary revolutionaries who choose the forms of organisation and the strategy of social change according to the specific conditions in their societies, and who by no means wish to imitate Stalinist Statism, have to clash both with internal conservative forces and their Western supporters, and with the *quasi*-socialist international establishments.

The international situation is indeed paradoxical. On the one hand, the struggle of the super-powers creates possibilities for the emergence and survival of socialist movements; in the absence of its Eastern rivals, the advanced capitalist world would have been able to suppress those movements much more easily. On the other hand, in the absence of the threatening Eastern Leviathan, socialist forces would have been much stronger within Western capitalism, and would have had much greater freedom of creative development elsewhere in the world. In this sense, the greatest enemy of socialism is the existing established world that labels itself 'socialist'.

Any sound contemporary theory of socialism cannot avoid two pertinent questions: How do you explain the bureaucratic deformation of initial revolutionary movements in Eastern Europe and by which social and cultural factors was it determined? What are the possibilities of evolution of existing Statism toward democratic socialism?

## 1  Social and cultural barriers to democratic socialism

A government can be overthrown within a couple of hours; a constitution and basic laws that determine a political system can be changed within a couple of months; an economic system can be dismantled and replaced by a radically different one within a few years; but even decades do not suffice to transform a culture, a set of deeply-rooted values, a customary pattern of behaviour, or a life-style.

Socialists seized power in a number of European countries between 1917 and 1945. They changed the institutions and built up new political and economic systems. But the original paradigm was distorted beyond recognition. Most critics – experts in anti-communism – begin by blaming the original paradigm for being unrealistic, utopian and naively optimistic about human nature. Certainly, each vision of the future tends to be unrealistic and utopian because it goes beyond the established framework, and tries to create new human forces for opening up entirely new possibilities. And human nature is by no means simply given, but capable of development in different directions depending on historical conditions created by man himself.

More sophisticated critics find essential faults with the nature of socialist organisations and movements. When socialists try to win power using the established, parliamentary, democratic machinery they must try and appeal to the middle classes and follow the rules of the established political game – which turns them eventually into professional bourgeois politicians. When they decide to violate those rules and seize political power by violent means, they cannot but create clandestine authoritarian organisations which, after eventual victory, give rise to powerful bureaucratic élites. The question of organisation is indeed the crucial problem of contemporary socialism, but it becomes so important only against a cultural and psychological background of an unstable, semi-developed, stagnating country.

Authoritarian forms of socialism developed first in those countries which geographically and historically belong to Europe and are heirs of ancient, rationalist, democratic culture and of the Enlightenment, but which missed the bourgeois democratic revolutions and entered the twentieth century as mixed, oriental feudal-bourgeois societies. Russia, Austro-Hungary, Prussia and neighbouring smaller East European countries were all politically and socially backward, absolutist and oppressive. But in contrast to non-European, ancient civilisations, they were committed to the ideas of individualism, material progress, industrialisation, urbanisation and violence as the most effective means of solving social problems. The result was a peculiar blend of European instrumental rationality and egoism with Byzantine-Oriental despotism without either typically European commitment to emancipation, or characteristically non-European moral and spiritual aspirations.

Socialism meant – for most of the people who supported it in these countries – an opportunity for accelerated material development. Humanist and democratic ideals were lost from the beginning; those who took these seriously were sooner or later eliminated as revisionists, renegades or traitors. Certainly a vague, unarticulated idea of social justice was always associated with socialism, but it was invariably spelled out in material terms: bread, land, the end of an unjust war and the end of foreign exploitation.

Abolition of poverty is certainly one of the major objectives of socialism. However, what is meant by poverty is not only material but spiritual poverty; not only a lack of objects owned, but also lack of needs; not only poor, limited, individual existence, but also poverty of collective, communal life-manifestations. Abolition of poverty in this broad humanist sense presupposes the existence of a society which has already developed productive forces to such an extent that the basic material needs of all can be met, a society in which a large part of the population has already satisfied its hunger for basic material goods and is ready to focus its attention on higher-level needs – for culture, communal life and creative activities. Eastern Europe was far from that condition when it became the stage for the first large-scale socialist experiment in history. Paradoxically enough, the socialist revolution had to play the role of a bourgeois revolution in opening the gate to an accelerated industrialisation and urbanisation. Instead of taking over an affluent economy, socialism had to try to produce one. With it, it also produced a typically bourgeois consumerist mentality – a formidable constraint to any humanistic socialist vision.

The grounds for this mentality existed even before exponential material growth was given top social priority. One of its roots is the typically European belief in material progress as the key to the solution of all human problems. Another is individualism, that derives from classical Greek culture. Consequently, having an increasing amount of goods, rather than being in an increasing number of ways, was broadly accepted as the road to happiness. And one had to travel that road alone, in competition rather than in solidarity and mutuality with other individuals. Instead of creating new forms of communal life, socialism in Eastern Europe tended to destroy old, traditional ones. These were predominantly rural societies with up to 80 per cent of peasant population. People lived in large extended families, in old village communities, attended local churches, respected traditional customs, were linked by the strong bonds of patriarchal morality and delighted in various kinds of communal festivities. Much of this social life was historically doomed: any normal bourgeois development would have uprooted most peasants, dispersing them into the cities, irradicating their patriarchal culture. And it would have offered them political parties, trade unions, city churches, humanitarian societies, independent cultural groups, or sports societies. This was clearly not enough to reintegrate the confused uprooted peasant-workers socially. The society that emerged in the wake of the socialist revolution offered even less: the chance of becoming a loyal employee of a State enterprise and of joining colourless and self-alienating political organisations.

The original socialist vision was distorted, not only because the leaders interpreted it in the wrong way and because their political organisations were authoritarian from the start, but also because of the human material which they presupposed did not exist in those societies at that time. Man, who by the force of economic and political measures was prevented from continuing his peasant existence, and who, once urbanised, isolated, was ready to undergo any hardships and deprivations in order to succeed and impress his former village with his new status and property, was an ideal builder of a bourgeois rather than of a socialist society. He needed commodities, and did not mind too much alienated labour and abstract, purely quantitative criteria of evaluation. He used every opportunity to get extra work and thereby extra income, and so did not have time to attend any meetings, except those which could promote his career. Such a worker does not struggle for his class interests, does not protest, organise or strike, he is the dream of every capitalist manager and, when his own socialist fatherland does not need him, he makes an excellent *Gastarbeiter*.

This is a possessive individualism without Western libertarian tradition. Most Eastern European States did not have the long history of free city communes, or independent, dignified burghers. Bourgeois democratic revolutions came late, and they failed. In Austro-Hungary, Russia, and elsewhere, there were despotic bureaucratic régimes which tended to reduce the citizen to an *Untertan* – a subject overwhelmed with the power of the State, ready to bow to every order, unaware of his civil rights, unaccustomed even to think that the State could be his own product, and its dignitaries regarded as mere civil servants. Socialism must take over where fully-developed, liberal bourgeois society stops. The principle of the sovereignty of the people has not only to be declared, but practically implemented; the domain of government has not only to be reduced, but replaced by self-government; public officials have not only to be elected, but also controlled, recalled and rotated.

Such a political arrangement requires a long democratic experience, such as that of the Netherlands, Britain, France or North America. Russians had that experience only between February and October 1917; some Yugoslavs between 1903 and 1914, Germans between 1918 and 1933, Austrians and Czechs between 1918 and 1938–9. The Hungarians and Poles by contrast had democratic movements and uprisings which contributed more to the formation of a free citizen's consciousness than brief interludes of a bourgeois democratic State.

There is enough evidence now to describe, in theoretical terms, what happens in the attempt to bring to life a socialist vision of society without previous democratic political culture. In the absence of civil liberties, social forces that struggle for the realisation of that vision are not able to create a broad, democratically organised movement, they are pushed underground, into small, clandestine, sectarian political parties ready to use violence in order to seize political power, and to use it as the basic instrument of social transformation. Such a Party likes to see itself as the vanguard of a revolutionary class, of an oppressed majority. But in reality this oppressed majority is not the proletariat and is not revolutionary, but is a peasantry and various middle-class strata. In the ideal case, as in Russia and Yugoslavia, they have indeed been disgusted with the old régime and have followed the self-appointed vanguard in the struggle for national liberation and for a more just society. In the difficult, turbulent times that begin after a successful political revolution the masses at best continue to follow, they never develop into a real historical subject. The goals look too vague and distant, risks too great, the sense of identity quite blurred for the whole, large, new group of peasant-workers, bureaucrats and employees of the bureaucratic apparatus. The most likely psychological phenomenon that now takes place on a large scale is 'escape from freedom'. The uprooted, isolated individual in search of social status and material well being frees himself from any social responsibility and follows the leadership – or at least does not oppose it. Thus Stalinism is not only the work of Joseph Visarionovich, or even of the bureaucratic élite that needed him, it is also the collective product of the confused, disoriented, 'little' man.

As Wilhelm Reich, Fromm and others have shown, the 'little' man develops in an authoritarian family. However, there are different kinds of authoritarian families. One that used to prevail in Eastern Europe was based on patriarchal tradition. The father was the unchallenged master over his wife and children. The behaviour of a woman was fully determined by an unconscious ideology according to which her natural role in society is one of housekeeping and child-bearing. Even to those women who actively engaged in the revolution and assumed important social positions, it never occurred to demand a just distribution of housework with their husbands. They expected help from their mothers, hired women-servants (contrary to all their emancipatory principles) or tried to carry both burdens: office and household, not counting political and other voluntary public activities. When they became exhausted they withdrew from politics and, whenever they could from work too. They would look for relief in sick leave, rescue themselves by early retirement or would play with all other possibilities except one – urging their husbands to share household work. Socialism, which was supposed to abolish any pattern of domination, stumbled at this most elementary social level. It met a pattern of domination, deeply rooted in a thousand-year-old family structure and ready to reproduce itself time and again. Basic education was in the hands of the woman-mother and teacher. She kept reproducing her husband in each boy, and herself in each girl. And both had to be obedient children, good pupils and loyal citizens – which had nothing to do with the socialist vision of developing free, independent, dignified self-determining personalities. The fact is that 'socialism' has nowhere succeeded in producing such personalities on a large scale. The second generation, born in socialism is invariably conformist. There are exceptions: the students who led rebellions in the sixties in Hungary, Poland, Yugoslavia and Czechoslovakia. They were under the fortunate influence of dissident intellectuals, great liberation struggles in the Third World and emancipatory youth movements in the West. But the scope of these movements was limited. It was young intellectuals who rebelled, hardly ever young workers and peasants. And much more than in the West, they expected their fathers and professors to lead them. Repressive measures against the older generation drove them into passivity.

In addition to possessive individualism, absence of democratic political culture and the patriarchal type of family, nationalism is another major cultural and psychological constraint to the realisation of humanist socialist vision.

All the major States in Eastern Europe – Russia, Austro-Hungary and Turkey – have imprisoned various national minorities. Poles, Czechs, Slovaks, Croats, Slovenes and Hungarians suffered under the Austrians; Serbs, Macedonians, Montenegrans, Bulgarians and Romanians were enslaved under the Turks; Ukrainians, Georgians and Armenians under the Russians. When these oppressive national conglomerations disintegrated by 1918, each liberated nation tended to create its own State, or at least developed an extreme sensitivity toward any tendency to re-establish the pattern of national domination in some new form. Bringing to life a truly internationalist, socialist vision, introducing for the first time a spirit of true mutuality and solidarity among nations proved to be an impossible task. Very early after the October Revolution, Lenin realised, much to his chagrin, that a chauvinist lurks within each Russian communist functionary. On the other hand, before Stalin brutally suppressed their national aspirations Georgians, under the brothers Mdivani, tried in vain to gain some autonomy from their northern big brothers. Neither one nor the other followed Lenin's formula, according to which formerly dominating nations were supposed to support every demand for self-determination, whereas formerly oppressed nations would be expected to advocate staying together.

In Yugoslavia a remarkable level of national solidarity was realised during the struggle against the common occupier and domestic Quislings. But as soon as the war was over, while the illusion still reigned that at last a genuine brotherhood and unity was achieved, Serbs, Slovenes and Croats started quarrelling about the allocation of scarce resources and federal support to conflicting plans of national economic developments. A quarter of a century after the victorious revolution – by 1970 – the conflict erupted in such an antagonistic form that it threatened to disintegrate the federation.

There is invariably a double cause of such conflicts. On the one hand, there is the inevitable rivalry among ruling élites, who regard their countries and peoples as their legitimate private property which has to be expanded and bolstered up by all means and, if feasible, at the expense of brother nations. On the other hand, there is a large-scale, typically middle-class resentment towards neighbours, a need for ethnical identity in an increasingly depersonalising technical civilisation, a romantic glorification of the distant past, and uncritical appropriation of old, mediaeval national folklore.

The sense of national belonging, no matter how great its mystification, is also a firmly entrenched reality, a hard empirical fact. This fact was largely underestimated, even light-heartedly glossed over in socialist visions. Yet it is a tremendous impediment to genuine international solidarity and mutuality that socialists always dream about. It can not only always reproduce old tensions and resentments, but also explodes into full-scale war – as recent events in South Asia clearly indicate. That nationalism is a curable disease – that it is not an inevitable human predicament, but a recent historical product – may be concluded from the fact that each new generation spontaneously tends to overcome national barriers and identifies itself with a broader, international community. Regrettably, the alliance of bureaucracy and conservative middle-class intellectuals usually succeeds in nationalist indoctrination and in diverting the attention of the young generation from social to national objectives.

The conclusions from preceding analysis are: first, in all countries of Eastern Europe where socialist visions were attempted for the first time in history, they met insurmountable cultural and psychological barriers in possessive individualism of an insecure petty bourgeoisie, and uprooted rashly urbanised peasants, in authoritarian political tradition, and in the patriarchal family and nationalist syndrome.

Second, these cultural and psychological constraints are the historical product of retarded and abortive bourgeois development, but instead of being removed they were reinforced by the new revolutionary establishment.

Third, the most conscious socialist forces themselves bore the mark of general social backwardness: they were organised in an essentially feudal, élitist and hierarchical way and never set an example of a self-determining, egalitarian community. Therefore, instead of coping successfully with all those overwhelming impediments they themselves continue reproducing them.

Fourth, what this world of 'real socialism' learnt from the more advanced industrial civilisations of the West or from non-European civilisations were some of their worst features. It accepted Oriental despotism and the Western ideal of an unlimited, wasteful material prosperity.

The bizarre mixture of those two, with some elements of socialist tradition, produced a relatively stable, viable, steadily growing society. But the gap between initial socialist ideals and the produced reality grew ever wider. Most of those problems which had plagued earlier societies survived or were reproduced in more drastic forms: economic inequality, political domination, violation of human rights, cultural stagnation, moral confusion, a consumerist style of life, privatisation of the individuals and mutual hostility among 'brother' States.

One strong source of legitimacy for all real socialist régimes was accelerated material development and a steady rise in the standard of living. A commitment to the fastest possible growth found its ideological basis in a simplified interpretation of Marx's theory. Marx saw in 'the growth of productive forces' the most dynamic factor in past history. And he is indeed responsible for an implicit illusion of unlimited progress owing to the unlimited wealth of natural resources. However, in Marx, technological progress has merely an instrumental character. 'The growth of productive forces' is a means of satisfaction of human needs, a means of possible reduction of working hours, and of a many-sided human emancipation. Once the followers of Marx established themselves safely in power, the means became an end in itself. A cult of material production gradually lost its earlier function of overcoming poverty, and of generating a basis for self-development of all individuals. The good life was reduced to a comfortable life, a wealth of needs to a need for material wealth – like any bourgeois society.

The new Statist society was not able to legitimate itself by meeting either the socialist demand for more social equality, nor even the customary bourgeois democratic demand for more political liberty. Its main virtue was its ability to produce goods and increase consumption. But the growth rate steadily decreased; and after 1977 the system found itself in serious economic difficulties. To some extent the present stagnation in the standard of living is the consequence of a world-wide economic crisis. Much more, it is the result of wasteful bureaucratic management, generally low work motivation, especially in agriculture, and high military expenditure. The overt response of people to such problems varies from country to country: from mass revolt, leading to a powerful oppositionary movement in Poland, to a widespread resignation that contributes to an impression of stability in USSR.

The crucial question is: is there a way out of Statism? All kinds of attempts have been made in the past: in Yugoslavia in 1948, in the German Democratic Republic in 1953, in Hungary in 1956, in Czechoslovakia in 1968, and in Poland in 1956, 1970, 1976 and 1980–1. What can be generalised on the basis of all those experiences about the historical possibilities of transcending Statism?

## 2  Armed uprising or reforms from above

One should, first, consider two simple opposing views – that the only road to liberation from bureaucratic shackles comes from an armed uprising; or that a social reorganisation and expansion of democracy can only come as a consequence of the liberalisation of bureaucracy.

The strategy of armed uprisings follows from three premises. The first is that bureaucracy is a new ruling class; the second that a ruling class would never give up its privileged position voluntarily; the third that the only way to deprive a ruling class of its domination and privileges is to overthrow it violently.

The first of these premises is dubious, the other two are

wrong. In contrast to other ruling classes the power of bureaucracy does not rest on property, but on function. Only through the managing function does it appropriate certain property rights, such as the free disposal of the State-owned means of production. But it lacks other property rights, for example, the right to alienate State property or to leave it in heritage. Since functions are not easily transferable, but can easily be lost at any major turning point, bureaucracy lacks stability and allows much more fluctuation than traditional ruling classes. Furthermore, while it has a strong sense of mutual solidarity in any confrontation with the people, it lacks a clear sense of identity, develops a tremendous amount of 'bad faith', and, in order to survive, has to hide itself behind the ideology of the working classes. It can offer its services to any régime, and therefore when under strong pressure of the people and especially when a national catastrophe is the only alternative, it is able to yield, at least temporarily. Abolishing the power of bureaucracy amounts to a true revolution, but not every revolution is violent and precipitous. A structural transformation could take place in any number of steps.

Two events shed considerable light on the issue of an armed uprising against Statist systems.

In July 1953 there was a mass workers' rebellion in Berlin, which spread to the whole territory of the German Democratic Republic. The rebellion was quickly and brutally crushed by the Soviet Army. It was spontaneous, and not backed by any strong background organisation: Germany was an occupied country, without much prestige in the world. Owing to the Cold War the rebels enjoyed some political support in the West, but under the circumstances any military intervention from the West was out of question: the uprising never had a chance.

Much more complex was the Hungarian uprising of October 1956. At that time, Hungary had the status of a 'people's democracy', but it had one of the most rigid and unpopular régimes in the whole of Eastern Europe just at a time when, after Stalin's death, a relative liberalisation was starting everywhere. Even when the hated Rákosy was dismissed under pressure from Khrushchev, he was replaced by an equally fanatical hard-liner Ernö Gerö, who ordered the army to open fire on the demonstrating crowds on 23

October. The rebels won the first round: Imre Nagy was appointed the new premier and promised important reforms; the Soviet troops evacuated Budapest on 27 October. There was a chance for democratic socialism at that point.

The Hungarian revolution coincided with a comparable revolt in Poland. The Soviet leadership was divided on the issue of intervention in these two countries. Nagy's government had the solid support of the working classes and intellectuals around Petöfy club and György Lukacz. It was possible to proceed with the reforms, to consolidate gains, and organise an overall self-defence against any foreign intervention. At that point Hungary needed an organised democratic movement comparable to Poland's Solidarity, and a mature and rational leadership that would proceed very tactfully and very realistically, at each moment aware of the limits of the really possible. Hungarian rebels transcended such limits in every direction. Workers spontaneously created self-managing councils – and not only in factories, but at the higher levels of social organisation. They went further than the Yugoslavs when they formed a central workers' council in Budapest. Such a council was an open challenge to the State and was the product of grass-root democracy. On the other hand, Hungary moved quickly toward a democracy of the Western type: political parties reconstituted themselves, a coalition government was formed, the released Catholic Cardinal Mindszenty, notorious for his collaboration with the pro-Nazi government during the war, was received in Budapest in triumph. On top of all that, Hungary announced its withdrawal from the Warsaw Pact. Soviet troops did not intervene in neighbouring Poland where Gomulka controlled the situation, but they did in Hungary where Imre Nagy was increasingly losing influence. What helped the Soviets to send their troops was the British-French attack on Egypt at the same time. The risk of open confrontation with the West was thus considerably reduced. It became quite clear that more than desperate courage was needed to resist a professional invading army. The static defence of cities, city sectors and particular factories was doomed from the start, it is a miracle that it lasted a fortnight. The guerrilla tactic of withdrawal and sudden attack over the whole country is probably the only one that ever has a winning chance under these circumstances. However, a process of rapid erosion of socialist forces was already underway in Hungary and, even in the case of a successful resistance, a development toward democratic socialism would have been less than probable.

This case study clearly shows what the pitfalls are of an armed uprising against Statism. It provokes a violent response in the whole supra-national system, and not only in the particular national régime. It attracts all oppositionary forces, not only socialist ones. The clandestine character of preparations invariably determines a strictly authoritarian character of organisations that lead the struggle and which would, in case of victory, establish themselves in power.

A directly opposite approach is an evolution from above. Roy Medvedev in his *Problems of Democratisation and Détante*[1] states this view very concisely:

> In such conditions [of great natural wealth, ability to grow continuously and to avoid any serious political or economic crisis] a reorganisation of social and economic management, an enlargement of political and civil liberties, an expansion of socialist democracy, can come . . . not as a result of open pressure by the popular masses and the intelligentsia but as a consequence of initiatives, from above (p. 19).

Medvedev clarifies his view by mentioning on the one hand, how the population 'below' is passive, silent, obsessed with a sense of guilt, how during the period of 'liberalisation' most intellectuals adopted a waiting attitude; and on the other hand, how most important changes, such as the exposure of the cult of personality of Stalin at the 20th Congress and the thaw after the 22nd Congress, were the work of the political 'heights'.

Passages like this leave the impression that the fate of socialism depends almost exclusively on the insight and goodwill of the bureaucracy. But there are also other passages which at least ask pertinent questions. Medvedev says, for example,

> But if today it is not the outlook of those 'below' that is of decisive importance but the moods and views of those above, how can the political heights be impelled to proceed not towards a further 'tightening of the screws' but towards an enlargement of socialist democracy?

Indeed which social forces are there that can impel the political 'heights' to proceed in one direction rather than the other?

At the very end of his article, Medvedev gives the credit to the new generation of leaders who now increasingly understand the need to improve the material living standards of the Soviet people. Then he adds:

> But the level of our production of spiritual values is extremely low, although the majority of Soviet people precisely regard spiritual nourishment as an ever more important component of their needs. At the same time it is obvious that without true democracy, without a free exchange of ideas and opinions, it is absolutely impossible to create any satisfactory spiritual values. Let us hope that in time all Soviet people, including the majority of their leaders, will make this simple truth their own. (p. 27)

We obviously have here a vicious circle. A high level of the production of spiritual values and a new humanist culture, are surely necessary conditions of socialism. This high level is impossible without true democracy. And, vice versa, true democracy is impossible without the previous creation of certain spiritual values, without a 'socialist enlightenment'. Where will this new culture come from? Is the only thing to do to hope that the leaders will eventually understand that they must introduce socialist democracy in order to ensure a high level of 'spiritual nourishment', to build up a genuine socialist society?

But are there any grounds for such a hope? And is it possible to do something in addition to hope?

One of the most naive and harmful prejudices in the contemporary socialist movement is the view that capitalism must inevitably be followed by a classless, Stateless, marketless, éliteless society, and that therefore the leaders of a contemporary social revolution, pushed by the iron hand of historical necessity, have no other choice but to build such a society.

However, social revolutions clear the ground for the realisation of more than just one historical possibility. In our time, they have mobilised all kinds of non-proletarian social groups, and their activists and leaders are very different kinds of people, who are apparently led by the same ideology, but interpret this ideology in very different ways and are actually motivated by very different aspirations. What is being described as the 'building of socialism' takes place in societies which still have a long way to go to get industrialised and urbanised, the political structure of which is below the level of eighteenth century bourgeois democracy, the culture of which is lacking in the great spiritual values of the epoch of Enlightenment, and is still permeated by authoritarian and patriarchal ideas and attitudes. Deep below the optimistic rhetoric of the leading cadres there is a sense of inferiority and insecurity. The new order must be preserved by force, it cannot offer either the level of material consumption or of civil liberties prevailing in the surrounding, supposedly historically inferior, bourgeois world.

What types of leader can be expected to grow under such conditions? All types in a large continuum between genuine revolutionaries, sincerely committed to the cause, to cold pragmatic rulers who could equally function in any society, to the ruthless, power-hungry autocrats whose vanity and egoism have no limits. From the objective conditions it will depend how great is the chance and how much time is needed to create a genuinely socialist community. From the outcome of the struggle among various factions within the presumably monolithic leadership, and especially from the way in which the popular masses react to the existing social conditions and initiatives for change, it will depend whether a post-revolutionary society develops into democratic socialism, a despotism of the Stalinist variety, some more liberal form of State capitalism, or any conceivable mixture of these three.

The official theory in the Soviet bloc is that communism will inevitably emerge as the result of the scientific and technological revolution. The element of truth in this theory is the fact that the development of productive forces really prepares the ground, and increases the objective possibilities for the transition toward a more human and democratic form of social life. But it does not guarantee such a transition. A high level of material consumption is compatible with extreme forms of bureaucratism. Catching up with America in wealth and comfort need not involve much progress in socialist democracy. Primitive, uneducated *apparatchiks* would certainly have to be replaced by highly skilled technicians; the whole process of management could be computerised without transcending its alienated, authoritarian character. While people are passive and apparently satisfied with being ruled, their rulers can hardly be expected to go out of their way and compel them to get free.

Obviously, in countries where a genuine mass revolution

took place some time in the past, the bulk of the working class and the intelligentsia has so fully and deeply adapted itself to the new régime that subsequent crises are never so dangerous, and the sense of alienation so acute as to give rise to an open rebellion. Here the latent dissatisfaction with some aspects of the system and the current policy finds various other ways of expression. These are not so stormy, violent or directly threatening as in the case of an uprising, but could be equally effective in supporting more liberal and progressive factions of political leadership, and in producing a series of desirable social reforms. This is, in fact, a mechanism of possible future democratisation of the Soviet Union with five basic factors in play: i) successful domestic policy, especially of economic development; ii) favourable international conditions of relatively stable peace and détente; iii) strengthening the internal position of a more liberal political faction; iv) the emergence of a new socialist culture that brings to collective consciousness alternative, more human possibilities; and v) the formation of a powerful, progressive public opinion that exerts pressure on the political leadership and slowly but irresistibly pushes it toward democratisation.

Meeting all these conditions is not very probable. Therefore, owing to its enormous natural resources and potential for economic growth, to its discipline and resignation of its people, the Statist system can survive for a considerable time even if individual nations (for example, Poland and Yugoslavia) overthrow it.

The Yugoslav case shows how far one can go by resolutely opposing the central power of the Statist camp, by explicitly challenging its ideology, and by introducing important reforms from above.

The Yugoslavia that broke with the Soviet leadership in 1948 was in every institutional respect a Statist society, a replica of the Soviet system. But it emerged from an indigenous, victorious liberation movement, enjoyed broad mass support and had a great sense of dignity. *Prima facie*, it clashed with Stalin over the issue of independence. Yugoslavs were not willing to tolerate a tutor. This in itself did not determine taking a different road to building socialism. At a deeper level, however, the conflict and its resolution were prompted by the essential contradictions between an ossified totalitarian system, and a young revolutionary movement that still had great emancipatory potential. It is true the Communist Party of Yugoslavia was a typical Leninist Party. But it led a vast movement which escaped its full control, which had to be decentralised to a large extent, and which was so successful precisely because it found a reasonable measure of both central direction and local autonomy.

The existence of a large number of young revolutionary cadres who had not passed through the harsh Comintern school before the war, and who took their ideals of social justice quite seriously, explains how it was possible to defy the towering authority of Stalin and the threat of Red Army intervention. The existence of the Cold War, and the geographical position of Yugoslavia, were favourable circumstances for the possibility of breaking away from the embrace of 'big brother'. However a decisive factor in this – and any other – liberation was the readiness to take the risk and to offer a most resolute resistance to outside intervention.

For a long time its leadership needed broad mass support, and consolidated it by introducing initial forms of self-management. The process of democratisation reached its peak at the end of the fifties and the beginning of the sixties. The State transferred many of its economic, political and cultural functions to a network of self-managing councils and assemblies. Alongside the flexible State planning, the market became a regulative factor. Civil liberties were brought to life to a remarkable degree. The Party was turned into a 'League of Communists', an essentially educational organisation. De-professionalisation of all politics was on the agenda. But the attempt to turn the Federal Assembly into a supreme, genuinely self-governing institution failed in 1963–1965. The limits of democratisation from above had been reached. Revolutionary leaders, turned professional functionaries, were no longer ready, twenty years on, to give up their unchallengeable power and undergo the customary democratic procedure of free elections, rotation and recall. Society thus stayed half way between Statism and self-government, oligarchy and democracy, political centralism and decentralisation, the plan and the market.

These were the full implications of a basic ambiguity inherent in the Yugoslav revolution from the start. The activists and soldiers of the partisan army fought for a free, just society. The leading cadres shared these goals, but assumed that the victory gave them a mandate to lead for an indefinite time. In fact they believed that the two were compatible. Self-management was not imposed on them under the pressure of the masses. They themselves reintroduced it: they found the forgotten idea in the literature after the break with Stalin, and created the appropriate institutional forms. But these forms lacked substance because true power remained in the hands of one hierarchical authoritarian organisation. The tacit assumption was that people would freely obey, continue to elect the same ageing leaders, give consent to all switches and turns of daily politics, and use the freedom of the press only for 'constructive' criticism. When harsher critical opinions were heard, opponents to professional cadres were proposed candidates, and a civil society began to reconstitute itself independent of party control, the entire process of democratisation was effectively blocked. The naive belief that self-government was compatible with one-party monopoly of power had to be given up. The illusion was replaced by a 'bad faith'. The seventies saw a proliferation of 'self-governing' institutions: commune assemblies, the delegate system, the disintegration of the federation into eight 'sovereign' States and eight autarchical economies, the disintegration of enterprises into 'basic organisations of associated labour', the building of an entire expensive, alternative apparatus of the 'self-managing communities of interest'. The net result of this frenzied effort was an increase in the number of clerical workers, and of wasting time and resources, rather than an increase of democracy. Present-day Yugoslavia exhibits the limits of democratisation 'from above'. It demonstrates that under modern European conditions a violent revolution led by a Leninist Party need not result in the cruelties of the purges and the *Gulag*, with the deprivation of human rights. On the other hand, it proves the following simple truth: the structure of human relations that prevails in the early cells of a victorious liberation movement will be projected and preserved in the final product of that movement: a post-revolutionary society, a State, an organised public life. No self-determination out of domination, no autonomy out of heteronomy, no justice out of inequality.

### 3   Democratisation under the pressure of an intellectual mass movement

The Prague Spring of 1968 is another case of attempted radical reforms of a Statist system by an enlightened party leadership. In comparison with Yugoslavia, Czechoslovakia had an important advantage: a high level of industralisation and of urbanisation, and a great democratic tradition. As in Yugoslavia and unlike other East European countries the Communist Party enjoyed a true mass support. (In 1946, in free elections it had emerged as the leading party, with 38 per cent of the total vote.) But there was no preceding revolutionary movement, no fighting experience, no strong will to oppose forcefully any foreign intervention and the geographical position made intervention highly probable. As we shall see, this turned out to be the fatal weakness of the entire Czech movement for 'socialism with human face'.

After Stalin's death and Khrushchev's revelations at the 20th Congress of the Communist Party of the Soviet Union, some demands for reforms were slowly formulated: more freedom of criticism, the rehabilitation of the victims of the Stalinist trials of 1949–1954, and economic reforms to end mismanagement and stagnation. The reformists within the Party gained momentum, writers, journalists and composers became increasingly more critical of dogmatism, party interference and the lack of liberty. The first anti-régime demonstrations took place in 1963. Novotny had to make concessions – censorship of the press was relaxed, as were the control of culture, and restrictions on travel abroad.

In January 1967 the 'new economic system', designed by Ota Sik and his team of experts, was implemented. The reformists within the Party were able to set up two working parties: one, headed by Radovan Richta, studied scientific and technological revolutions, and prepared the paper *Civilisation on the Cross-Road*. The other, under Zdenek Mlinarz, studied *The Development of Democracy and the Political System in a Socialist Society*. While slowly preparing some reforms Novotny's régime tried, at the same time, to compel the mass organisations to conform. This only heightened tension, especially between the Party and the increasingly rebellious students and writers. The crises, – economic, political and moral –

culminated in 1967. At the Fourth Congress of the Writers' Union extremely sharp critical speeches were delivered by Vaculík, Klima, Liehm and others. Since the censor forbade their publication they were duplicated and distributed illegally. In the autumn of 1967 students' anger because of poor life conditions erupted in a mass demonstration in Prague. Eventually, the Party reformists toppled Novotny and on 5 January 1968 Alexander Dubček became first Party Secretary.

This was not only the victory of the liberal faction of the Party over the conservative faction, but also the triumph of the mass alliance of intellectuals and workers. What united them was a revolt against despotic rule, suppression of legality, mock trials, mistreatment of political prisoners, violation of civil rights, censorship, bureaucratic planning, wrong investment policy, inefficiency, and stagnation of the economy.

Within this broad alliance there were some tensions. The new leadership was most interested in the liberalisation and modernisation of the economy, decentralisation of planning; rehabilitation of the market mechanisms; changes in the patterns of investment (switching from heavy industry toward more production of consumer goods); greater role of well educated, technocratic cadres, and of 'scientific management'. The kinds of reform, resembling very much the Yugoslav 1965 economic reform, constituted much more the reintroduction of certain elements of liberal bourgeois rationality and efficiency than a radical breakthrough toward a new economic democracy. Its concerns were not issues of vital importance to the workers, such as social equality and worker participation in decision-making. In fact Dubček's government refused both to remove the old bureaucrats from central ministries, and to have workers and peasants on governing boards. Equally reluctant were the Party liberals to accept the basic demands of the intellectuals including freedom of the press and of organisation, autonomy of culture, and the democratisation of all political life. Censorship was abolished, since the liberals still needed open criticism of the conservatives, and of Novotny, who preserved some power as the President of the Republic. But they had mixed feelings about the growing freedom of speech and press which escaped any Party control. Dubček, Černík and Svoboda were virtually dragged along by the mass movement. What they intended was to transfer the exorbitant powers of the State to an élite of well-educated managers. However, the workers demanded self-management. When, on 5 April the Party adopted this demand, an attempt was made to implement it in the form of industrial councils which would include, alongside workers' representatives, State representatives, outside specialists and representatives of 'general interest' (customers and suppliers). Less than two months later, on 1 June, another project for 'workers' councils' was adopted. This did not give much power to the councils, either. The latter had the right to nominate the director but not to take decisions itself. The first detailed project of workers' self-management was prepared by the Wilhelm Pieck factory workers on 29 June. A truly revolutionary democratic movement gained more and more momentum, especially in the period between May and August. It was leaderless and pluralistic since various political currents reappeared that were earlier forced into silence. But it had potential for a radical structural transformation of Statism. Precisely for this reason the country was invaded by the Warsaw Pact armies on 23 August. However, the workers' councils continued to grow even after the Soviet invasion. In January 1969 a 'council of councils', with delegates of about 200 firms from all over Czechoslovakia, assembled in Skoda factories in Pilzen.

What made the invasion and subsequent return to Statism possible was not only the overwhelming military power of an integrational bureaucratic alliance and the fact that the world military balance was already disrupted by American intervention in Vietnam, but also the extraordinary weakness of the Czech leadership, which made two fatal blunders. One was the refusal to resist the invading armies, the other was the acceptance of the offer to form a government in the occupied country. The opposite was necessary: a total rejection of any collaboration with the occupying powers, and, even more important, the resolute preparation for self-defence immediately after the overthrow of Novotny. The Czech people lost an extraordinary opportunity because they tried to resolve an essentially moral issue by logical reasoning, and in addition made tremendous errors in that reasoning.

Whether to defend freedom and justice or accept slavery is a moral issue, and has to be solved independently of any analysis of the situation in terms of the strength of the enemy and likelihood of outside aid. Even the most peaceful movement for revolutionary change must, from its first day, prepare to defend its achievements most resolutely and, if necessary, most forcefully. The Czech State already had a good professional army. In addition an armed self-defence organisation of the entire people for a partisan war was necessary. But an analysis that appeared to be realistic turned out to be unpardonably naive. The Czech leadership did not prepare its defence because it did not really believe in the possibility of intervention: now we know better. Furthermore, it was foolish to assume that the stronger side in a conflict would attack merely because it was stronger, and that, therefore, an 'objective' analysis in terms of numbers and material forces would suffice to answer the question whether it pays to resist or not. In fact the stronger opponent also has to take risks and to pay the price if it comes to fighting. And he also must ask the question: if a strong resistance can be expected, will it pay to win or not? A resolute determination to resist may discourage the aggressor. This proved true with respect to Yugoslavia in 1948–49, and with respect to Poland in 1956 and 1980.

## 4 Democratisation as the result of a workers' movement

In many ways the Polish struggle against Statism deserves special attention. It is the most resolute one and flares up with increasing determination every few years, in spite of all sacrifices. It is most complex, and involves Party members, liberals, ardent Catholics, nationalists and internationalists; it rejects socialist ideology explicitly, but at the same time preserves basic socialist values. It is by far the best organised and, in contrast to all other similar movements in Eastern Europe, it has been led by a large, truly workers' movement. What is most important of all, while in other comparable cases we are examining tragic episodes of past history or, in the case of Yugoslavia a static situation holding out only slim chances of further democratic development, what we have in Poland is an open, dynamic, extremely promising process: a true history in the making.

The 1980 crisis in Polish society has deep roots and more than one dimension. While predominantly economic, it is also moral and it broke out against the background of a traditional, national conflict and the imposition of a régime with which the vast majority of Poles were not willing to identify.

Statism has generally been regarded as a symbol of Russian domination in Poland. Russia has been the traditional enemy since the fourteenth century. At first it was the object of invasion – Poland occupied White Russia and the Ukraine, and, in 1610 even held the Kremlin for a brief period – then was a formidable aggressor, beginning with the Thirteen Years' War, 1654–67. Poland has been divided by Russia, Prussia and Austria three times (1772, 1793 and 1795) until it was completely wiped off the map of Europe for more than a century. Two risings against Russian rule, in 1830 and 1863, were brutally suppressed. All education and government were Russified after 1864. Eventually, the Poles regained independence after the overthrow of the Tzar at the end of the First World War. However, Polish workers and peasants did not greet the Red Army as a liberator, spreading the revolution westwards, but as a dangerous conqueror. This led to the bloody Polish-Soviet war of 1920–21. Another partition of Poland by Nazi Germany and the Soviet Union in 1939 did not help to reduce hostility. And it was further intensified by two other events: the disappearance of 14,300 Polish officers, who were taken prisoner of war by the Soviet army and executed in Katin; and the total passivity of the Soviet Army near Warsaw while the Nazis were destroying the flower of the Polish youth during the sixty-three days of the Warsaw uprising in August-September 1944.

Eventually, Poland was liberated by the Soviet Army. But the new régime was not freely chosen by the majority of Poles themselves. Polish communists valliantly fought against the German occupying forces, but considerably stronger forces in the underground movement were pro-Western. For that reason the Polish People's Republic found itself in a political and moral crisis from the very beginning. Most people had to live in a system which was not of their choice nor the product of their own history, or even something to which they reluctantly gave consent. With foreign troops on their soil they could not have faith in their institutions, and could not believe in the meaningfulness of what they were doing. A sense of absurdity reigned not only in the theatres, but in social life at large. Leaders never had much credibility; political organisations never gained mass following. The relations with the Catholic church were strained, especially in the early 1950s. Most Polish intellectuals did not even try to adopt Marxism. Even the pro-Moscow Communist Party functionaries were opposed by a strong 'nationalist' faction. Workers' rebellions erupted at increasingly briefer intervals: 1956, 1970, 1976, 1980.

These rebellions were prompted by the systematic failure of the authorities to supply enough food and consumer goods at tolerable prices. An ambitious industralisation programme, with a strong emphasis on heavy industry and an export drive, produced shortages in consumer goods and indirectly affected agriculture. Polish leaders were wise enough not to collectivise the land (less than 20 per cent was in collective or State farms by 1954). However, the peasants were not stimulated either materially or politically to increase their production. In 1955 agricultural production hardly exceeded the absolute amounts of grains and livestock produced in 1938. Since 1953 Poland has had to import about one million tons of grain annually, and this did not suffice. In 1956, the Poznan workers' first demand was for bread. But in addition they also demanded free elections and the departure of Russians. The return of Gomulka brought about a temporary relaxation, but did not substantially change either the system or its policies.

After 1970 the new Gierek government reversed the economic policies. It raised huge loans from the West and invested them in light industry, with the intention of improving the standard of living. It succeeded initially. But investments were not made rationally enough, the amount of waste was staggering; corruption assumed massive proportions. The moment of truth came in 1980. By that time Poland's national debt exceeded $20 billions and the world bankers were willing to continue with loans only under the stipulation that the government undertake a resolute stabilisation policy. As a consequence, heavy subsidies on the price of meat and other foodstuffs were removed. Workers in Gdansk and Szczecin reacted with a general strike.

All three preceding workers' rebellions involved violent

clashes with the police and hundreds of deaths. This time the
workers organised themselves, and, very carefully and wisely,
aware of the limitations of the entire Polish society, formulated their demands. Firmly, but also patiently, they negoti-
ated with the governments' representatives. Their organisation, Solidarity, spread over the whole country and by 1981
embraced ten million workers.

This is an essential innovation – not only in post-war Poland
but in the entire history of humankind. No other country has
seen a spontaneous grass-root workers' movement of this size
emerge so quickly without the tutorship of a political party or
trade union bureaucracy.

Another crucial innovation is the alliance between intellectuals and workers in which the former do not even try to
assume the traditional roles of leaders and masters-thinkers.
Intellectuals have worked hard over the years in establishing
personal links with the workers. And when the storm erupted
they modestly offered their services: knowledge of facts,
analysis of past experiences, articulation of basic demands and
aid in negotiations. They came as close to Gramsci's description of 'organic intellectuals' as anything in European history.
This was especially surprising since Polish intellectuals have
always distinguished themselves by a tremendous sense of
pride.

Another unique Polish phenomenon, impossible anywhere
else in Eastern Europe, was the very possibility to organise
outside of official frameworks. It is true that the Poles found
suitable forms: KOR was initially only a committee for
workers' defence. Solidarity was only a non-political trade
union organisation. But the government was not exactly a
paradigm of tolerance. There were arrests and harassment.
But while Polish activists were by far bolder and more determined than any other East Europeans, the Polish government
was also more liberal and tolerant than the authorities anywhere else in Eastern Europe. Of course, a tough government
would have been able to prevent the development of the
reform movement. But then, in all probability, this would
have left violent revolt as the only way out.

In addition to this new character of a worker-intellectual
alliance, Solidarity exhibited several other striking features.
Without being a peasant party, it embraced hundreds of

thousands of individual farmers; without accepting Marxism or even explicitly subscribing to socialism, Solidarity attracted a majority of Party members. And it embraces 90 per cent of practising Catholics, although its basic values are more in the socialist than in the Catholic tradition.

Polish peasants now have a Solidarity organisation of their own, which demands control of the land, national liberation, and is against war and feudal and bureaucratic injustice. In the past free individual farmers have either supported a petty-bourgeois political party or created their own peasant party. Agricultural workers employed by farmers have sometimes organised into trade unions. But there was never a farmers' trade union which joined a large workers' union, sharing with it common goals.

Further, there was never a Communist Party that would undergo a fundamental reorganisation under the impact of an outside opposition movement most of whose members would identify far more with that opposition than with their own Party. The leadership of the Party did not go as far as the Yugoslavs in 1958 in accepting an entirely new, non-ruling, educational role (a decision which, after all, was never fully implemented). But their real structural reforms, introduced at the July 1981 Congress, were quite impressive: leaders were made truly responsible to the rank and file, they were elected in genuine secret elections, freedom of criticism was fully tolerated, and the horizontal committees within the Party involved an amazing level of pluralism.

The Catholic church played a very important role in the emergence of Solidarity. Being in opposition to the régime, it offered all the advantages of a powerful organisation outside the system – space, equipment, the means of communication. The fact that a Pole had become Pope and was head of 750 million Catholics round the world, also offered an impressive protective shield. Whatever the record of the Catholic church as a source of inspiration in the struggle against established earthly powers, in Poland it had an important spiritual effect on its congregation. As a bearer of traditional national values it was a cohesive factor. And it prevented demoralisation, cynicism and apathy: customary phenomena among uprooted peasant-workers and consumer-oriented middle classes in societies of this type.

The amazing achievement of Solidarity – that it attracted more than ten million Poles of all strata and creeds – can be explained by the fact that it was not led by any vanguard political organisation and lacked any ideology. It does not yet have any elaborated programme; there are programmes of Kuron, Mychnik and others. It does not subscribe to one definite model of development: a plurality of aspirations still waits to be brought into a coherent whole. But it would be too simple to say that opposition to the régime is the only common denominator of all members of Solidarity. There are many elements of a general programme in the initial twenty-one demand of the Gdansk workers: (i) *civil rights* – the right to organise independent trade unions, to strike, freedom of the press, full religious expression, the release of political prisoners from the 1970, 1976 and 1980 uprisings; (ii) *economic* – the reduction of wage differentials by a substantial increase to lower pay groups and the reduction of salaries and privileges of top functionaries and managers; increases in pensions, more food in the shops, a decrease in the waiting time for housing, a five-day working week; (iii) *social* – trade union participation in economic decision-making; higher professional expertise rather than political suitability of managers; reduction of retirement age, better health care provisions; more nursery schools for the children of female workers. These are all typically liberal-socialist demands, but since everything was done in the past in Poland in the name of socialism, the term is unpopular and discredited. The people do not even wish to distinguish between 'good' and 'bad', 'authoritarian' and 'democratic' socialism. They try to speak a new language which is not ideology laden.

However, when one studies various programmatic texts that appeared during Solidarity's first year of existence, one detects the following basic values: social justice, equality, individual liberation, the right of participation, freedom of communication and democratisation of social institutions. These are not the basic values of Catholic Christianity, although early Christianity is one of their sources. In fact, these values constitute the central core of contemporary humanist socialism.

Disagreements arise about their implementation. How is democratisation to be understood? Does it mean a return to the *Szlachta* (gentry) concept of democracy? Or adoption of a parliamentary multi-party system? Or some new combination of immediate, participatory democracy, and representative democracy? How should the *Sejm* (assembly) be constituted? Should it have one or two chambers? (One for the representatives of Solidarity, the other for the representatives of the Communist Party.) However, what is not contentious is that all elections should be free, with several candidates amongst whom to choose; that workers' self-management ought to be introduced in all enterprises; and that the State apparatus must be reduced to a means of permanent social movement. Among economic ideas within Solidarity there is a consensus that planning must be decentralised, that State ownership must become true collective ownership, and that private ownership must be recognised in agriculture and small-scale production. All this proves that even Solidarity's boldest ideas are not really anti-socialist, as the Warsaw Pact press keeps repeating.

The crucial issue that looms large over the Polish scene is, will the Soviet Army intervene? It did in East Germany in 1953, in Hungary in 1956, in Czechoslovakia in 1968, and in Afghanistan in 1980. Why not in Poland?

If anything can be generalised about Soviet foreign policy, then the rules seem to be: (i) The Soviets try to make sure that there are friendly, co-operative régimes in neighbouring countries ('Finlandisation'); (ii) The Soviet Union is ready to 'defend' any of the socialist régimes in Eastern Europe from their own people ('proletarian internationalism'). Since Poland is on the Soviet border and is facing a probable radical change to its system, there is indeed the permanent possibility of Soviet military intervention.

Both the Party and the State have lost a good deal of credibility and authority in Poland. The truth is, of course, that they never were too high – with Soviet troops on Polish ground. One leader who symbolised the struggle for independence, Gomulka, turned out to be a poor, unimaginative, inflexible leader; a middle stratum of firmly entrenched Stalinist cadres effectively blocked any reform. Factionalism and corruption reigned in the Party heights. Since Autumn 1980, the Party has remained in power only because the workers are sophisticated enough to know that they must proceed slowly, and not provoke the USSR.

However some credit for the Polish miracle must go to the Communist Party in Poland. Like the Yugoslav Party it has some tradition of opposing the Comintern dictate, which is why it was dissolved in 1938. While some leaders (e.g. Bierut and Jaroszewicz) stayed in the USSR during the war and returned to Poland with the Red Army, others (e.g. Gomulka and Moczar) led the Polish partisans; there was always tension between the two wings. Many Polish communists took part and died in the 1944 Warsaw uprising while the Soviet troops watched from the other side of the river Wisla. The Polish Party never became merely a symbol of foreign domination, and never resorted to such brutal measures in the consolidation of its power as were used by some other East European régimes. It was reluctant to follow the Kronstadt example whenever riots exploded.

The Party's attitude has indeed been ambiguous. Orders were given to shoot in 1956, and workers were killed in Poznan; and again in Gdansk in 1970. And yet the workers' protests were not dismissed as counter-revolutionary (as in Kronstadt, Budapest and elsewhere) but were recognised as legitimate grievances. The Party took a part of the blame on itself and the leaders had to go: Ochab in 1956, and Gomulka in 1970. Edward Ochab deserves to be remembered as the only leader in any European Communist Party who not only admitted his own responsibility and incapacity to cope with the situation, but who also on his own initiative, released the more able man from prison – Gomulka – to replace him.

Since 1956 the Polish Party has gradually learnt that of the two possible strategies for the resolution of the conflicts with its own working class – brutal suppression or compromise through negotiation – the latter is by far more preferable, even if it involves some agonising reappraisal of its own limitations and the giving up of excessive power and material privileges. As the early days of Gomulka, Gierek and Kania's régimes demonstrated, it was possible to regain some credibility and popular support. On the other hand, an oppositionary movement gave a better bargaining position and some degree of independence with respect to the Soviet leadership. It was easy for Khrushchev to dismiss such unpopular leaders as Rákosy and Ulbricht; but with respect to Gomulka he was helpless.

The economic reforms of Gierek, and the reorganisation of the Party under Kania, were not met with strong Soviet opposition precisely because they went half way towards resolute public demands.

There were three moments between August 1980 and August 1981 when even some of the most sophisticated observers of the Polish scene felt that the course of events would lead to Soviet military intervention. One was the first explicit demand to create a mass organisation (a free trade union) outside the political system and independent of the Communist Party. The second was the extension of Solidarity to embrace individual farmers. The third was the democratisation of the Party in the July 1981 Congress, which more than decimated old professional cadres and affirmed the principle of the democratic election of the leadership.

A specific form of the domino theory was behind such analysis. Any of the achievements of the Polish workers would allegedly destroy the authority of the Party beyond tolerable limits. The Soviet Union would have to intervene, otherwise the system would collapse in all Eastern European countries. These would be won for the West, and the Soviet Union itself would be weakened beyond repair.

There are fundamental errors in this reasoning. After all the concessions were made and reforms implemented, Kania's Party, in August 1981, enjoys more prestige with the Polish people than Gierek's in August 1980. Polish events are not some kind of virulent bacteria that infects neighbouring Statist countries. They are unique products of a uniquely Polish development. Workers elsewhere do not have the same historical experience, courage and maturity, or comparable connections with intellectuals. The economic situation that prompted the unrest differs essentially from that in neighbouring countries. Other Communist Parties did not pass out of the same school between 1956 and 1976.

Even the worst warmongers, who were able to argue in 1956 and 1968 that Hungary and Czechoslovakia were becoming a vacuum to be filled with Nato troops, know very well that Poland, in contrast, has no borders with the West, and is surrounded by Warsaw Pact countries; this allows a higher degree of tolerance on the part of the USSR.

There are other reasons for the Soviet reluctance to interfere in Poland with arms too. One is their engagement in Afghanistan since December 1979. The political price of that intervention is especially heavy: further damage to their international reputation, condemnation by 104 countries in the United Nations, disapproval of many Communist parties, irreparable damage to détente, and the reduction of trade with the USA and the West. Another reason is that even in the case of a most favourable outcome, (i.e. the destruction of any opposition and political stabilisation) the Polish economy, with its enormous national debt, annual deficits, food shortages and poor motivation for work, would become an intolerable burden.

And a favourable outcome is far from certain. Once General Jaruzelski declared that 'the Polish soldier would not shoot at the Polish worker' it became more likely that an intervening army would meet the resistance of all patriots, rather than provoke a civil war between 'socialist' and 'anti-socialist' forces. Given the enormous courage and determination of the Polish people, any outside intervention would lead to a horrible bloodbath.

Solidarity can diminish the likelihood of such an intervention even more if it makes in advance all the necessary preparations for national guerilla resistance.

In the absence of outside military intervention an interesting situation would emerge in which all three parties involved would have to learn how to resolve conflicts in a non-violent way. Workers would have to proceed slowly and patiently along the road to reforms, renouncing the immediate realisation of all their demands. The Polish Communist Party must learn to yield its monopoly of power, and to rule with the workers not against them. The Soviet Union will have to learn to have in its neighbourhood a system that is essentially socialist, but incomparably more democratic than its own.

Some analysts believe that the most difficult problem for the Poles in the immediate future will be restoring an economy in shambles.

In another country, a movement like Solidarity could begin to disintegrate for economic reasons. Prolonged disorder and growing scarcities of basic goods does in fact sometimes bring about mass nostalgia for a firm hand. That is how the fascist régimes emerged; and that is how De Gaulle returned to

power in France after the collapse of the entire social fabric in
May-June 1968.

In Poland economic difficulties still serve to keep the
movement growing and the social transformation going on.
Once the desired democratisation is achieved and the meaningfulness of work and the sense of national and human dignity restored, a rise of productivity and an intelligently
restrained consumption will be able to lead the country out of
its present crisis. Poland has important natural and human
resources: it is rich in fuels (a net exporter of energy), could
considerably increase its food production, and has an impressive scientific culture.

Another difficulty in coming months will be the maintai-
nence of a necessary minimum of unity and discipline within
Solidarity. It is now a huge, pluralistic organisation expressing
various interests, lacking a common programme, and facing
inevitable struggles between its various factions. The especially dangerous moment will be the transition from a control
and critique of governmental policies towards assuming greater responsibility for determining policies. That ethnic
homogeneity is a great advantage for the Poles one can easily
realise by having a look at the Yugoslav scene. Besides, one
may hope that those who have learnt to lead in dialogues with
the enemy, will know how to do so with friends – although the
history of sectarian struggles within socialist movements is
not reassuring.


## 5 Conclusions: from Statism to Democratic Socialism

The transition from Statism to democratic socialism involves
the abolition of bureaucratic power, a restructuring of all
institutions and a democratisation of all spheres of social life.

In some respects it is more difficult to abolish bureaucracy
than the bourgeoisie; in other respects it is easier. It is more
difficult for at least the following five reasons:

(i) The bourgeoisie, as a class, can be abolished by one single
act: the socialisation of the means of production. In contemporary advanced industrial society capitalists are no longer
indispensable either as organisers of production or as rulers of
the country. The former function is already being performed

by managers, the latter by professional politicians. Bureaucracy of the Soviet type directs both and, before it can be removed, an alternative self-governing structure must be ready to replace it.

(ii) The bourgeoisie can be overthrown since it does not immediately control the apparatus of force; during a crisis some parts of that apparatus may turn against the régime. Bureaucracy controls the Army and the police and does everything to strengthen them for its protection. Furthermore, it has a monopoly of all mass media and uses it in order to present itself as the subject of revolution and the defender of national interest.

(iii) Once bureaucracy succeeds at least partially in identifying itself with socialism, the power of workers' councils, integrity of the country and internationalism, then each rebellion against bureaucracy attracts all counter-revolutionary, racist, chauvinist and clericalist forces. Therein lies the danger of a movement that follows an absolute principle of negation, that challenges all existing institutions without any qualification, and intends primarily at destruction, leaving the building of new forms out of the ruins for a later moment. Abolition of State property could give rise to private and group property, bureaucratic planning could be replaced by a *laissez-faire* free market, one party by multi-party professional politics, centralistic integrity by disintegration across national, racial and religious lines, bureaucratic waste by individual consumerism.

(iv) In a primitive society without a democratic tradition an oppositionary movement is likely to have an authoritarian character and merely reproduce a bureaucratic structure.

(v) Any régime in trouble counts on support and aid from similar régimes. A bureaucratic régime is far better protected than its bourgeois counterpart. Here an intervention across State lines has its full ideological and political rationalisation ('communist solidarity', 'proletarian internationalism', 'the Brezhnev doctrine').

On the other hand, the domination of bureaucracy is less stable than that of the bourgeoisie. It needs secrecy and ideological mystification because it lacks real legitimation. It disguises itself with the slogan of the power of the working class, it hides its operations behind well closed doors, it conceals its wealth and privileges, it prevents freedom of the press and of organisation because it knows it could not survive open criticism and a legal opposition. Modernisation undermines the very basis of bureaucratic existence. It tends to overcome all artificial barriers and to built big systems in the entire civil society. Bureaucracy is indispensable as long as the civil society is non-existent (as in Soviet Union) or disintegrated (as in Yugoslavia). In the former case all public life is turned into political society; in the latter case it is artificially split into small systems and bureaucracy is needed to co-ordinate it. As I have argued in earlier chapters, the necessary measure of co-ordination may be achieved in far more efficient and democratic ways if a minimum of political decisions are taken by democratically-elected representatives, leaving technical decision-making in the hands of those who have the necessary knowledge and skills. There is no ground, then, for the existence of a special group of self-appointed professional rulers who are neither specially qualified nor truly represent the general will of the people. When this becomes clear, bureaucracy can continue to rule only by the threat of violence and owing to a complete demoralisation and apathy of former revolutionary forces. As we know from the history of Russia, China or even Austro-Hungary such states of social stagnation can last for years, decades or centuries. When it comes to human subjectivity there are no reliable predictions. However some tentative generalisations can already be made about the conditions which must be met for any promising attempt of emancipation from Statist shackles.

The first condition is existence of a profound crisis of the system that brings into question the legitimacy of the ruling élite not only in the eyes of some intellectuals but of the population at large. This crisis is not only economic: the main reason for East European revolts since Stalin's death and Khrushchev's revelation was the consciousness of the despotic, unjust, immoral character of the power. When economic difficulties begin to play a crucial role, as in Poland, it is not so much the general state of the national economy that matters, but the state of micro-economics: of individuals, families and communities. The national economy may be in a shambles, but individuals or particular sectors of the economy may still enjoy large accumulated reserves (as in Yugoslavia in 1980–1981). Conversely, the national economy may be in good shape, but a growing number of individuals will revolt against personal deprivation and injustice. A crisis with explosive political potential begins only when a large mass of people begins to believe that life is miserable because the ruling powers are ignorant and dishonest, and that there is a way out.

Another condition of possible liberation is a split within the ruling bureaucracy itself. We have seen that in Yugoslavia, Poland and Czechoslovakia. From the start, in the wake of a victorious revolution, a process of polarisation begins between the idealists, utopians, 'the beautiful souls', who truly believe in building a free and just society by honest means, and the realists and pragmatic politicians who accept that you cannot be a revolutionary and keep your hands clean. The latter use and reject the former. But another phase of polarisation takes place within the latter group. Some are still seriously committed to their original goals, although they believe that these justify any means. Another group are primarily motivated by personal power, wealth and the good life. They are bright, ambitious individuals from the lower classes who find every other avenue to social promotion blocked, and who become revolutionaries because this is the only available means to achieve their ambitions. Under different circumstances they would become tycoons, generals in professional armies, prime ministers in bourgeois cabinets or heads of the Mafia. It turns out that, with considerable luck, a revolutionary career will open access to all desirable 'goodies'. For these leaders initial revolutionary goals remain at best a means.

By the time a revolutionary vanguard turns into a ruling bureaucracy, it is this last group that is firmly in saddle. It has no scruples and it will use revolutionary violence mercilessly to get rid of any opposition. This is the 'party of the order', the centre of all 'hard-liners'. On the other hand, idealists (for example the workers' opposition in USSR) or practical revolutionaries still committed to the revolutionary ideals of their youth (for example Trotsky, Bukharin, Zinovyev, Kamenev and Kyrow), will either be purged as 'fellow travellers', or physically liquidated. Those among them who agree to serve will either be morally destroyed and turned into cynics, or split, following the official line, blaming themselves, but secretly preserving some partial identity with their initial project. They become a natural centre of a 'liberal' faction within the Party.

Younger cadres who join the leading élite are either ruthless careerists themselves, convinced that force and brutal pressure resolve difficulties most efficiently, (to be sure, these will join the hard-liners) or, if they are softer, brighter, better educated, they will prefer more civilised methods of problem-solving, and will join the 'liberals'.

Naturally, things are more complex in each individual country. There are shades of grey between these extremes. There were at least three different kinds of 'liberals' in Yugoslavia after 1948. First, those who seriously committed themselves to the development of self-government (1950–1965); second, those who supported economic liberalism (1965–1972); third, those who, after 1972, continue to oppose excessive repressive measures and who occasionally speak out about the greater need for democratic dialogues.

Clearly, the concept of liberalism in this context is quite broad and covers many nuances between full support for civil and human rights on the one hand, and some weak resistance to bureaucratic terror on the other.

In normal times, hard-liners and liberals manage to agree on basic political issues and to unify against any radical opposition to the régime. They begin to differ more sharply at the time of deepening crisis. The party of order sees only one remedy: the strengthening of security forces, blaming imaginary foreign and internal enemies for the poor performance of the system, and crushing all opposition by brutal force. This sounds suicidal to the liberal faction. Sheer survival instinct leads it to look for reforms. If there is a strong social movement demanding social changes, the liberal faction will be the only one able to negotiate and preserve the basic structure of the system, in spite of all concessions. That is why it has a winning chance over the conservatives. We have seen this in Hungary in 1956, in Czechoslovakia in 1968, in Poland in 1956, 1970 and 1980.

Once the worst of the conservatives disappear from the scene, some liberals themselves begin to play a somewhat conservative role: they try to oppose popular pressure, and save as many structural features of the existing system as possible. They begin to divide amongst themselves: the

Svobodas and Dubčeks, who have to be pushed on the one side, the more radical reformists like Smrkovský, Mlynář Pelikan and Černý on the other. The *status quo* faction led by Gomulka prevailed in Poland in 1956, and the radical transformation of Polish socialism was contained without outside 'brotherly aid'. The radical reformists, tremendously supported by growing intellectual and workers' movements, prevailed near the end of the Prague Spring in 1968. The decisive victory over Czech bureaucracy was eventually turned into defeat only owing to the Soviet invasion in August 1968.

What we see now in Poland is one rebuff after another to the Party conservatives. The elimination of Grabski and of most professional cadres from the Central Committee of the Polish Party at the July 1981 Congress means nothing less than a decisive historical defeat of Polish bureaucracy. If one could disregard external circumstances, one might already conclude that the Polish working people could seize basic levels of power at any chosen moment.

The third essential condition for liberation from Statism is clearly the existence of a broad democratic movement of manual and intellectual workers. The peasants are the reserve army of such a movement. In Poland, for the first time so far, they are actively engaged and organised as a part of Solidarity. In other socialist countries they are critical of the régime even when they stay passive. Clearly, they will never accept the compulsory collectivisation and, even when they stay individual farmers, they can hardly identify themselves with a system that constrains them and exploits them in so many different ways. Peasants remain loyal supporters of the régime only when they have freedom to stay on their land and to freely exchange their goods in the market. This requires a system of the Yugoslav type. All systems of the Soviet type can never count on the full loyalty of the peasants.

The hardest question of all is: how is a broad democratic movement at all possible in a repressive State? None ever existed in the Soviet Union, Bulgaria, Romania, East Germany, or even in Yugoslavia after considerable liberalisation during 1953–1968. It only began to develop in Hungary in 1956, it flourished once only in Czechoslovakia in 1968, and twice in Poland.

When we analyse these cases we find that four essential

requirements were met in all of them.

(i) What preceded the constitution of the movement was invariably intellectual ferment: radical criticism of the official ideology and of the least rational and tolerable aspects of the system, revival of the basic values of a democratic and egalitarian political culture.

(ii) The students' movement radicalised abstract intellectual demands and provided initial practical energy.

(iii) The movement reached decisive strength only with the massive engagement of the workers. Workers protest their poor conditions of life, demand the right to organise, strike and participate in decision-making. Any violence on their part provokes brutal repressive measures. Nevertheless, at least in Poland, it was not entirely counterproductive: it gave rise to a self-criticism within the Party, weakened the hard-liners and brought about important cadre changes. However, workers achieved much more when they organised themselves, undertook well co-ordinated strikes, and began to paralyse the entire economy of the country.

(iv) The régime was neither able nor willing to go very far in using force. This hesitation is a very complex phenomenon. Among the initiators of the movement we observe an enormous determination, and readiness to take any risk – to lose employment, go to gaol, even be killed. People were indeed fired, arrested and killed. The security forces did not suffer from sentimentality. Political leaders, however, were not ready to persist in that direction. They were neither as fanatical as the Bolsheviks nor found themselves in a comparably desperate situation as the one in Russia at the time of the Kronstadt uprising in March 1921. Inner differentiation within the Party here plays an important role. All factions easily agree to fight the opposition. They also agree to respond with violence to workers' violence. But it is difficult to reach consensus and continue to kill when the workers march, organise, strike and call for negotiations peaceably. It is a question of human decency, of historical responsibility, of political realism (keeping at least some bridges unburnt), of unpredictability of all the consequences of mass terror. Once negotiations start, the Party faction that endorsed them has every reason to make them succeed. Their success does not only strengthen the liberal party faction, but also allows the movement to spread by leaps and bounds.

These movements are rare in Eastern Europe because all the four requirements are so rarely met at the same time. The Soviet Union has dissident intellectuals. There are some great literary and scholarly names among them and they are not inferior in courage to their Polish colleagues. But even the best students, let alone workers, are apathetic, quietly alienated, and more or less adapted to the system. There was significant unrest among Moscow students in 1956; there were waves of worker strikes. But these were not co-ordinated, and it was never easy even to be informed about events in various parts of such a huge country. Oppositionaries and rebels were treated with the traditional harshness of Ivan the Terrible and Peter the Great. In these high offices the 'soft' creatures, called elsewhere liberals, hardly ever survive. As a consequence, changes, when they must come, take place in violent convulsions. When Lenin and his comrades were sent to Siberia it did not look at all probable that a few decades later the Tzar would be overthrown by them. What plants will grow one day from the seeds sown by present-day dissidents, no one can tell.

Under such difficult conditions the question of tactics does not even arise. But when we examine developments in more civilised States, in Czechoslovakia in 1968 or in Poland in 1980 we realise that good organisation and appropriate tactics were of essential importance. The development of Solidarity will remain a paradigm case.

First, the small, independent, clandestine organisation of the workers led by Lech Walesa, and a committee for the defence of workers led by Jaczek Kuron were created. A bridge between the intellectuals and the workers was established from the start. The crucially important achievement was that such illegal organisations preserved the spirit of democracy. They avoided the temptation to develop an authoritarian leadership and of assuming the role of a vanguard. The great lesson is: the initial cell of the movement must not pretend to be a vanguard, a special organisation within the movement with special responsibilities and rights to hegemony. It must not be anything but the initial mover.

Second, the moment for action and of mobilisation for the movement must be well established: in Poland it was an extremely unpopular increase in the price of basic foodstuffs.

The action is non-violent: a series of strikes or protest demonstrations.

Third, while a huge organisational effort is made the authorities are invited to negotiate. This leads to differentiation within the Party, and gives a chance to the liberal faction, if there is one. If there is none, or if the childish pride of the rebels makes them refuse 'mere talks', and reject 'compromises' in advance, they are certainly doomed sooner or later.

Fourth, the decisive issue is how to avoid a violent intervention of one's own domestic professional army, let alone outside interference. For a long time it was believed that no significant social change was possible while the army was intact. Trotsky and Parvus were the first amongst communist leaders to indicate that the professional army must be seriously weakened through a defeat in war or in some other way, before consideration of the possibility of an armed uprising. Essentially, they were right. But the initial organisation of Solidarity did not stage an armed uprising. It did not even come up with a radical programme. Nor did it claim political power. It did not challenge the Army, the existing system, the leading role of the Communist Party, existing foreign policy and international obligations. The decisive demand was the right to organise in a non-political, trade union organisation. That was extremely heretical, but not provocative to the point of justifying shooting the workers.

Fifth, once the first round of negotiations has been won and the freedom to grow into an independent mass organisation secured, there is no hurry to formulate a common, long-range political programme. Such a programme would have scared and unified enemies, it could, on the other hand, divide and mutually alienate allies. Unity is preserved in essentially negative functions: those of watching, controlling the government, expressing concrete demands that can be met, without destroying the system, revealing the essential limitations of existing policies. The movement grows without focusing its attention on how to seize power.

Sixth, the first positive structural demand is workers' power in the enterprises. The participation of workers' delegates in the government comes later.

Seventh, while making an effort to win support in the professional army, the movement creates its own self-defence:

an overall organisation for guerrilla resistance.

Eighth, while everybody suffers from the effects of a profound economic crisis, the movement does not hurry to contribute what it can to its overcoming. It could offer constructive ideas, it could help to tighten discipline, stop strikes, increase productivity, persuade workers to acquiesce to the fall of real wages for the good of the country. That would eventually stabilise the system with some limited gains for the workers. However, if the system is to be slowly restructured, if reforms are to be revolutionary, the crisis will be allowed to take its natural course in the conditions of a class struggle and not in those of a class harmony. The existing authorities carry the responsibility for the poor functioning of the system. When the economy grinds to a halt everybody will be convinced that radical structural changes are necessary. The rulers will no longer be able to rule, the people no longer ready to live in the old ways.

This is walking a slippery tightrope. The risk is that the people might not endure the hardships and might turn away from such a demanding movement. They have done that in the past. So far the Poles have not lost their enthusiasm. They rebelled because of the meat shortage, but now independence and justice seem to them much more important.

In those golden hours of history when united human beings engage for credible, meaningful purposes all the laws and predictions of reifying thought break down. In quite a few countries poorly equipped ordinary people endured against formidable professional armies. Yugoslav partisans endured against an enemy who threatened to kill hundreds of helpless people for each lost soldier. Some of this spirit is indispensable for any significant emancipatory breakthrough in history.

## Notes

1　Roy Medvedev, 'Problems of Democratization and Detante', in *Détente and Socialist Democracy*, (Ed.) Ken Coates, Spokesman Books, 1975, (pp. 9–27).

# Index